BIG DATA
APPLIANCES
FOR IN-MEMORY
COMPUTING

Big Data Appliances for In-Memory Computing

A Real-world Research Guide
for Corporations to Tame and
Wrangle Their Data

Dr. Ganapathi Pulipaka

Published by High Performance Computing Institute of Technology

ISBN-13: 9780692599570
ISBN-10: 0692599576

About the Author

GANAPATHI PULIPAKA is a distinguished technology leader providing innovatory solution architecture on SAP Business systems, Enterprise application development, design engineering, management, and consulting delivery services offers expertise in SAP delivery execution and executive interaction as a trusted advisor. He started his career as an SAP ABAP Programmer. He has implemented around 25 SAP projects for Fortune 100 corporations and various other clients in the past 17+ years on next-generation SAP Applications providing a comprehensive portfolio of consulting solutions. He worked for 21 global corporations implementing SAP projects in building Global COE for SAP ERP, CRM, SRM, SCM, PLM, PPM, and BW NetWeaver products. Ganapathi Pulipaka is an SAP Certified Professional.

Ganapathi Pulipaka is research scholar in Computer and Information Systems who holds a Professional Doctorate Degree in Information Systems and Enterprise Resource Management from California Intercontinental University, Irvine, CA.

Preface

BROADLY DIVERSIFIED BIG data appliances like IBM DB2 Blu acceleration, Oracle Exadata, and SAP HANA compete with their ubiquitious capabilities for a blended database business intelligence system that can entangle online analytics processing and online transaction processing on the same platform that is big-data ready and an enterprise-ready solution. The role of SAP HANA is pervasive on emerging growth of technologies, medical Internet of Things, speech-to-speech translation, and neural networking processing of the events. SAP HANA is a multitenant database that can resolve complex conundrums of business analytics by handling super-extreme operational workloads. An independent qualitative research with new analysis buoyed by large-scale secondary empirical data from SAP interviews and highly structured survey results from IDC reveals that SAP HANA performance benchmarks from automotive, consumer goods and beverages, healthcare, government services, high tech, and public sector industries surpass classical relational database management systems in many ways. The purpose of the study was to explore the big-data appliances that diffuse the speed of big data to the organizations with awareness, interest, trial, evaluation, and adoption. Recommendations are provided for SAP HANA about (a) alternative future memory technologies to reduce the cost of infrastructure; (b) complexity of IT landscape; and (c) how SAP HANA can shape the future of emerging growth technologies such as medical Internet of Things and speech-to-speech translation.

Acknowledgements

I WOULD LIKE TO thank the leading research scholars of Information Systems, Dr. Robert Burdwell, Dr. Steven Hess, Dr. Kim Fields, Dr. Sally Lozada, and Dr. Andrea Clarke for providing their deep insights to further enrich the subject. All of the mentioned scholars have given deepest appreciation and love for the beauty and finesse of this subject.

Table of Contents

Table of Tables

Table of Figures

1

Introduction

CONVENTIONAL DATABASE TECHNOLOGIES in the marketplace today that are offered to enterprises are unable to provide a solution for faster access to data, unlike SAP HANA (Systems, applications, and products - High-performance analytic appliance). SAP HANA is an in-memory computing platform developed by SAP (Systems, applications, and products in data processing). The purpose of the present qualitative SAP HANA study was to research big data technologies that are early adopters, to analyze their smart computing capabilities, and to make recommendations for building a cost-effective and efficient big data solution.

Background of the Problem

The term big data refers to colossal volumes of data with different formats of data types. Delving into the intellectual evolution of big data, databases, relational databases, and in-memory databases provides insights into the information explosion of massive quantities of data. Heimer noted that SAP uses the term information *explosion* interchangeably with SAP HANA as a customer reality and consumer relationship to information technology (IT). Conventional sources of data such as academic journals, books, and newspaper articles historically served as sources of data. However, the evolution of the Internet has led to a new form of digital artifacts spanning a variety of data types such as online blog posts, digital articles, and websites.

The book *The Scholar and the Future of the Research Library. A Problem and Its Solution*[1] is a discussion of the growth of American university libraries based on the growth of the available data in the world. Sheldon and Moore[2] predicted the libraries would double in size every 16 years, and that the Yale University library will reach 200 million volumes by 2040. Sheldon and Moore also predicted that the shelves would occupy 6,000 miles of length in the library. The first time the term *database* was coined was when Sebastian and Coleman[3] asserted, "to capture the sense that the information stored in a computer could be conceptualized, structured, and manipulated independently of the particular machine on which it resided."

During the current decade, there have been two popular databases that revolutionized commercial use of database applications. These were network models on data systems language (CODASYL) and the hierarchical database model information management system (IMS). The International Business Machines Corporation (IBM) introduced semi-automated business research environment (SABRE) database system for the use of reservations data at American Airlines. It was a commercial success.

Price[4] proposed the law of the exponential increase. According to his prediction, the growth of scientific knowledge would double every 15 years. Price[5] also predicted that every half-century would see an increase in knowledge by a factor of 10, which would tremendously increase the number of scientific journals and papers by an equivalent factor. Codd[6] published *A Relational Model of Data for Large Shared Data Banks*, which led to the start of relational database models. Codd defined the logical database schema that laid out the cornerstone for relational database models to the world. In 1974, the University of California at Berkeley funded the relational database product Ingres that uses query language (QUEL). IBM funded the relational database product System R with a structured English query language (SEQUEL). System R subsequently led to the creation of competition with Microsoft's structured query language server (MSSQL) as well as Oracle Sybase products. During this time, the relational database management system (RDBMS) was widely recognized.

In the 1980s, structured query language (SQL) became the standard query language for a large number of the relational database management products. IBM introduced database two (DB2) as their robust version of relational database management. In the 1990s, the object database management system (ODBMS) was created. Subsequently, a golden digital era began with the advent of the Internet in the mid 1990s. Data grew exponentially as an increase in the variety of data types in online transactions resulted. In 1998, Mashey[7], a chief scientist at Silicon Graphics Incorporated (SGI) presented a paper entitled *Big Data and the Next Wave of InfraStress* at a Unix users group (USENIX) meeting. In the paper, Mashey presented and discussed different data formats such as audio and video, and the exponential growth needs of data on physical storage systems and the needs to extract the data per user expectations. Mashey discussed terms such as big memory and microprocessors, big net, bigger disk data, huge data, and technology change rates.

In 1998, Coffman and Odlyzko published a paper entitled *The Size and Growth Rate of Internet.* They predicted that the Internet traffic would overtake voice traffic in the US by 2002 based on the sizes of the network.In 2000, Lyman and Varian[8] at the University of California at Berkley published a paper entitled *How much information?* They discussed the information stored and processed by the population in exabytes per year. They presented the medium required for storage of data such as paper, film, optical, and magnetic storage. Following in 2001, Laney in 2001, authored a paper entitled *3D Management: Controlling Data Volume, Velocity, and Variety.* These "3VS" have become the standard for big data in the next decade.

For the first time in history, in 2007, EMC sponsored a data prediction research project. IDC (International Data Corporation) published a white paper *The Expanding Digital Universe: A Forecast of Worldwide Information Growth through 2010* with the predictions of worldwide information growth through 2010. In this paper, IDC estimated that information would grow by six-fold to 988 exabytes. In 2012, Gartner for the first time included in-memory database management systems and in-memory analysis in its latest research hype cycle report. Gartner has categorized these terms under emerging growth technologies as trough of disillusionment, meaning which the terms overhyped. Gartner predicts by 2017, in-memory database management systems will reach maturity by hitting the plateau of productivity. In sum, the need for data storage and management continues to grow exponentially since the advent of computers creating an ever more dire need for effective management tools.

Problem Statement

A review of the empirical literature revealed an incomplete and unbalanced body of knowledge about the cost of managing computer generated data, which is very high with minimal rewards as traditional relational database management system (RDBMS) tools cannot provide what real-time data customers need in the immediate moment. An ever-faster, big data explosion is occurring globally. As a result, organizations are unable to access the needed data to tap into the right opportunities to deal with complex problems relevant to informed decision-making. Lack of access to critical data based on analysis of corporate data creates missed opportunities to take necessary action either to introduce a new product, improve an existing product, or build the capabilities of the organization.

Most NoSQL (Not only SQL) tools focus on master data attributes. Organizations need to analyze their transactional data that is integrated with real time. Real-time integration is difficult with enterprise resource planning (ERP), customer relationship management (CRM), supply chain management (SCM), product lifecycle management (PLM), and supplier relationship management (SRM) systems. A tool is needed that can effectively process billions of records on Apache Hadoop Enterprise Edition and provide integration with all SAP business applications. In sum, organizations need data in real-time to be able to respond to market opportunities and globally there is a need for faster analysis of data.

Organizations would prefer the ability to evaluate multiple data sources and targets at once to convert non-standardized SAP formats into SAP format, and the ability to easily integrate with SAP stack of NetWeaver and Business Suite applications. To compete and outperform SAP HANA and Oracle Exadata big data analytics solutions, IBM launched IBM PureData. IBM strategic acquisition of Netezza Corporation for $1.78 billion in November 2010, which has shaped the future for catching the intense increase of big data in the marketplace. One solution is IBM DB2 BLU acceleration that embraces the data analytics for columnar database storage with actionable compression, dynamic-in-memory caching features to analyze the compressed data. IBM PureData aims for software and hardware integration with cloud computing capabilities with Apache Hadoop Enterprise Edition. The New York Stock Exchange (NYSE) Euronext Inc, T-Mobile, and Premium Healthcare Alliance are few clients of IBM PureData, which was implemented to disentangle their biggest challenges with big data. Now, IBM is in negotiations for big data investment with Aspera, an extreme speed file transfer company with the *fasp* protocol that can transfer files from cloud to cloud. It closed the acquisition in early 2014. IBM has spent over $16 billion in the past five years solely on analytics acquisitions.

Organizations need, but do not yet have, the ability to crunch through billions of records with enablement of big data integration and SAP business applications. IBM DB2 BLU acceleration solutions can integrate with SAP business applications. However, it is not enterprise-ready, and not big data ready. A separate software product, IBM PureData, was leveraged for integration with Apache Hadoop Enterprise Edition software. Multiple database products create complexities, lack of economies of scale for enterprises to run two software products for big data, and business information warehouse (BW) analytics.

Oracle offers Oracle Exadata software and hardware integrated with a single machine for extreme speed BW analytics in what Oracle claims is Speed of thought analysis. In November 2013, Oracle released big data appliance X4-2 for big data on Apache Hadoop Enterprise Edition. Oracle Exadata can integrate with SAP applications. However, it is not pure columnar database based model. Oracle leverages hybrid columnar compression method which is a combination of both columnar and row-based compression techniques still leaving a limitation.

Purpose of the Study

The purpose of this qualitative SAP HANA study based on second-ary data was to analyze industry trends of SAP HANA performance benchmarks. The study was focused on resolving performance challenges, reducing the complexity of IT landscapes, more efficiently moving data from online transaction processing (OLTP) systems to online analytic processing (OLAP) systems with flexibility, and resolve the global challenges of information delays in academics, aerospace, automotive, consumer products, food and beverages, government, healthcare, and utility. The objective was to analyze and present information with which to determine if (a) SAP HANA has addressed the speed, accuracy, and granularity, and the diffusions of the big data via awareness, interest, evaluation, trial, and adoption, (b) SAP HANA has efficient in-memory technology and architecture to blend OLAP and OLTP on a single strategic database system compared to big data appliances such as Oracle and IBM, and (c) SAP HANA has shown promising results in revolutionizing emerging growth technologies such a mIOT devices and speech-to speech translation. Data was obtained via SAP performance benchmarks. SAP research indicators measure SAP Performance benchmarks.

Organizations are looking for a reduction in cost of technology, infrastructure, and augmentation of business value delivered from in-memory computing. These benefits for businesses provide a quantum leap in terms of velocity, variety, and value. When an organization implements a competency center for data analytics, big data tools reduce costs. An in-memory computing tool is needed globally that can eliminate multiple third party vendors. An in-memory computing platform can unify the system integrators for integration towards SAP enterprise resource planning, supply chain management, customer relationship management, product lifecycle management, supplier relationship management, and data warehousing. This integration aims to solve the biggest conundrums of the organizations. The intent of the present study was to explore multiple big data tools with in-memory technology capabilities by drawing comparisons with best practices to see which best suits the industry.

Significance of the Study

The present study was undertaken to study evolution of the next generation of big data and how SAP HANA's research business cases can fuel various industries and shape the future of in-memory computing. Results suggest techniques to boost performance to ultra-blazing speeds. Results also suggest methods to bring data *in the moment*. Based on results, corporations in highly competitive environments may be able to position themselves strategically to illustrate how faster, bigger, higher performance of data can lead to more timely informed decisions. Results also contribute to the body of literature with development of performance benchmarks of SAP HANA against other big data technologies in the marketplace. Such developments may lead to boosting the diffusion of the big data industry and improve the adaptability of the product. Future studies may benefit from finding alternative solutions for in-memory solutions by going beyond dynamic random access memory (DRAM).

Research Questions

The fundamental purpose of this qualitative SAP HANA study was to analyze industry trends based on SAP HANA performance benchmarks. The following research questions were used to guide the methodology of the study, which will be found in Chapter 3:

RQ1: How can SAP HANA speed up the diffusion of big data via awareness, interest, evaluation, trial, and adoption?

Typically, adopting classical disk-based databases have introduced performance challenges due to the complexity of IT landscapes. Classical RDBMS databases have many systems supporting OLTP and OLAP processes. Therefore, there is complexity of the landscapes. The performance challenges stem from the fact that when there are so many systems, the data extraction, transformation, and loads have to occur between multiple systems; hence, there will be performance challenges. This is where SAP HANA may be efficient to move data from OLTP to OLAP, as SAP HANA is a blended database management system that can embed both OLAP and OLTP on the same platform.

RQ2: Why is SAP HANA more efficient than other big data appliances such as Oracle and IBM?

SAP HANA may be the technology to resolve performance challenges, reduce the complexity of IT landscape, efficiently process OLTP and OLAP systems with flexibility, and resolve global challenges of information delay. SAP HANA has shown the ability to have the blended OLAP and OLTP on a single database system by saving the transaction and automatically populating the content for business intelligence reporting purposes. Twenty-one percent of respondents of a research survey conducted by IDC responded that it is a complex challenge for business to move data manually between OLAP and OLTP. Oracle has hybrid row-based, columnar-based in-memory database. IBM DB2 Blu acceleration has column-based storage. However, it lacks the big data enterprise-ready solution for the ability to connect and transfer big data. Oracle runs Exadata on hybrid memory such as flash and DRAM with hybrid compression columnar-based and row-based storage. Oracle Exadata has industrial algorithms for database operations. However, they do not scale up to IBM DB2 Blu acceleration in-memory database industrial algorithms.

RQ3: What data show that SAP HANA can shape the future of emerging growth technologies?

Results of the study may show how mIOT and speech-to-speech translation can revolutionize the information technology with SAP HANA (mIOT is an emerging growth technology). Case studies are included in the discussion of this aspect of the research. The research pertinent to this question was intended to resolve performance challenges, reduce complexity of IT landscapes, more efficiently move data from OLTP to OLAP with flexibility, and reveal how speech-to-speech translation with IVR can resolve the global challenges of information delay.

Assumptions, Limitations, and Delimitations

Assumptions

SAP HANA based on a single database instance is clustered in-memory computing technology. The customers that are implementing SAP HANA first need to be Unicode enabled. To leverage SAP HANA, the database must be Unicode. Per IBM, SAP HANA requires proprietary hardware to run a database. However, IBM DB2 Blu acceleration in-memory does not require new proprietary hardware.

Limitations

The IBM DB2 Blu acceleration solution has actionable compression that means it does not require decompression during a query execution. However, SAP HANA requires decompression during query execution. This is compensated by *insert only on delta* mechanism of SAP HANA.

Delimitations

The present study does not highlight the composition of project teams and management aspects required for implementing SAP HANA solutions. This research effort did not provide the capital and operational cost associated with migration of existing infrastructure and databases to SAP HANA by industry.

Definition of Terms

Definitions provide specific, clear meanings of terms and thoughts without discrepancy[9]. Definitions provide concepts using theory, ideas, and structural meanings Ambiguous concepts and terms may influence the outcome of the research study. The following are terms mentioned in the current study:

Big data. The term big data refers to colossal volumes of data with different formats of data types. SAP uses the term *information explosion* interchangeably with SAP HANA as a customer reality and consumer relationship to information technology (IT).

Exponential increase. Price proposed the law of the exponential increase, which was that the growth of scientific knowledge would double every 15 years.

InfoCube. An object that can act as both a data target and an InfoProvider.

InfoProvider. An InfoProvider is an entity for which queries can be created or executed in BEx. InfoProviders are the objects that are relevant for reporting.

In-memory computing. A database management system that reads and writes from the main memory of CPU.

SAP HANA. SAP HANA is an in-memory computing platform developed by SAP (Systems, applications, and products in data processing).

Summary

The background of literature behind the present study was outlined, as well as the problem and subsequent purpose of the study. The research questions, which were based on the purpose of the study and the review of literature in Chapter 2, were cited. Assumptions, limitations, and delimitations were summarized. Chapter 2 contains a thorough review of the literature concerning the background of the issue of management of big data. Chapter 3 contains a discussion of the methodology of the data collection and analysis. In Chapter 4, the findings, of the study are presented. Chapter 5 consists of discussion of the results as they pertain to the research questions and recommendations for future studies stemming from this research effort.

2

Review of the Literature

THIS CHAPTER CONTAINS a comprehensive review of literature pertinent to SAP HANA. The exigencies of SAP HANA are reviewed
and how the process pushes limits to reach faster and higher performance in prevailing systems. SAP HANA provides insights to customers to improve products and services within organizations. Such
insights work to strategically position in the marketplace that allows
them to soar above the competition. Big data analytics provides the
impetus to create a wave that can result in epochal productivity and
output in the economy of nations. An example of this increase in
output was cited by the McKinsey Global Institute (2014). McKinsey
Global Institute asserted after an independent research project that
there will be a substantial rise in the gross domestic product (GDP)
in the US from 0.8% to 1.7% by 2020.

Documentation

The literature review facilitates creation of new knowledge by
providing and integrating accumulated knowledge in the area

of study under consideration[10]. Results of the review were used to establish that the topic of the study under review has never been empirically researched, and further, provided a foundation upon which the statement of the problem and resulting research questions in Chapter 1 were grounded[11]. The literature review facilitates creation of new knowledge by providing and integrating accumulated knowledge in an area of study. Chapter 2 is a summary of excerpted information from books, articles, and government documents that provide past and present information necessary for the research study on SAP HANA. The review adds to the current literature as it entailed an encompassing search and documentation of relevant knowledge from New Scientist magazines, IDC research, McKinsey Global Institute independent research, IBM research, Gartner research, Hasso Plattner research, SAP research, e-Books, Stanford University libraries, Oracle white papers, Dissertation databases Online Library for scholarly, peer-reviewed articles. The Internet was also searched for information and articles from Aerospike database, SAP HANA community, SAP HANA blogs, SAP SAPPHIRE ASUG conferences, Information Week magazines, IBM data magazines, InfoWorld magazines, New York Times newspapers, blogs, IBM Red books, IBM database library, and Couchbase white papers. The Google Advanced Scholar search engine was a source for Internet searches important to the topic. The literature review covered a total of 13 books, 163 peer-reviewed articles, and 58 organizational websites.

Historical Overview of the Problem

Similar to the evolution of Intel Pentium I to i7 core processors that boosted performance of systems, and the single core central processing unit (CPU) to quad core CPUs, the *Intelligent Economy* requires a groundbreaking evolution of a new database tool that can solve complex problems. Historically, SAP has been the business information warehouse accelerator (BW) with an accelerator suite solution entitled the SAP BusinessObjects Explorer. In the past, for open connections and heterogeneity, SAP has provided an accelerated version of SAP BW with integrated caching. Still needed is a significant and revolutionizing change in the system that requires in-memory computing technology.

SAP NetWeaver BW initially had information models with dimensions, also known as star schema tables, that could aggregate and classify characteristics under one-dimension table that grouped multiple Stammdaten Identifikationsnummer (SID) tables. The dimension table represents a single model, but also runs on the traditional database. A SAP HANA attribute view can be reused for multiple purposes with master, or transactional data attributes at blazing speed.

SAP BW was primarily built to connect to an SAP ERP system, and for every 50,000 SAP ERP customers there were at least 13,000 SAP BW customers who bought and implemented SAP BW solution. However, customers have been experiencing latency problems with SAP BW as some of the extractors run for 48 to 50 hours before extracting the data from SAP BW extractors. The system is flooded with many background processors when extractors are running. Due to the resource intensive consumption of the system, SAP BW extractors have required multiple splits to run the SAP BW extractors. The SAP BW solution was only built as a core SAP BW solution to support majority of customers running SAP ERP systems. The lack of heterogeneity in SAP BW system does not allow efficient integration with non-SAP data, (unstructured, semi-structured data) to process gigantic volumes of big data. On the timeline of SAP acquisitions, in 2010, SAP's acquisition of Sybase has revolutionized the way SAP research labs are investigating how to build a roadmap with their own patented database technology. Based on the background of data processors and advances in the quantity of information making its way into the realm of cyberspace, the following section is a discussion of the future of big data.

The Future Involving Big Data

When Rider in 1944 predicted that the growth of libraries would double every 16 years, Rider did not consider the new digital era of books in a new electronic format such as e-books and audio books. Rider did not consider storage devices such as disks, hard tapes, flash memory, solid state drives, or cloud computing. Since Rider's predictions, new platforms have been created every decade bringing continual revolutionary change in the way organizations conduct transactions. Big data analytics appliances such as SAP HANA and Apache Hadoop have been distributed across platforms such as cloud computing and the Internet of Things (IOT) shaping the future of industries like retail, manufacturing, healthcare, government, and supply chain management. Organizations are currently taking a leap of faith with the advent of the new digital age by converting the raw and crude data from anywhere into something refined and advanced in a fraction of a second. Given the future of big data, a discussion of the potential for its management in the marketplace follows.

The Potential of Big Data

Big data analytics is predicted to evolve as a significant catalyst in retail, manufacturing, health care, and government services. The retail and manufacturing industry sector is expected to grow and contribute to the GDP by $325 billion by 2020 with big data analytics. Significantly, there is an expected increase of $285 billion of productivity and change in output of GDP by 2020 in the health care and government services industry sectors. According to an IDC report, the world's data is projected to rise to 40,000 exabytes of data by 2020.

The incendiary cloud computing has revolutionized the data migration from private to public clouds and vice versa. IBM is working on a cloud-of-clouds solution that will allow anyone to move data seamlessly from any cloud to any other cloud, which will allow the movement of big data from cloud to cloud with ultra-blazing speed. However, Hewlett-Packard (HP) and Red Hat already have such a solution in the marketplace. In addition, IBM is on the verge of introducing a cross-cloud communication conceptual framework with high-security encryption despite moving data from one storage product to another.

IBM's big data investment company Aspera's *fasp* file transfer service can enable the big data to travel at an unprecedented speed of 24 GB (Gigabytes) per 30 seconds. With these extreme speeds, the intelligent economy is gearing towards massive processing cloud computing power for the next frontier of innovation and competition. Big data is expected to raise productivity in the retail industry mainly in three sectors: supply chain management, global operations management, and production of commodities. With ultra-blazing speeds of the big data revolution there is a projected growth expectation in materials management, carriage and freight management, disputes and collections management, advanced returns and complaints management, and employment workforce. The retail sector is expected to have a boost of $30 to $55 billion in GDP growth with the evolution of big data.

In the manufacturing industry sector, the consumerization of data leads to research and development of new products or improvement of existing products. This sector of industry is expected to gain by $125 to $270 billion. Bloom noted that big data from various data analytics contribute to the rise of this industry sector.

Electronic medical records are a catalyst for the healthcare industry. Big data flows through electronic medical records into the healthcare industry. It is contended that this is beneficial for diagnosis, augmentation of financial management, informed decision-making, analysis of medical equipment usage, and improvement of deeper market penetration strategies. The data tsunami of big data is expected to improve the healthcare industry in terms of healthcare best practices, safe drug administration, disease control, and informed decision-making. The big data analytics of the healthcare industry are expected to save $100 to $190 billion dollars.

The efficient analysis of the massive data volume in government sectors could generate cost savings up to $95 billion. This can be achieved by automating the manual processes with big data and monitoring the data transactions in volumes that can lead to informed decision-making. Bloom concluded Federal agencies in the government are turning to big data to improve the tax system and augmentation of quality auditing. The Internal Revenue Service (IRS) was able to save $2 billion with big data analytics from 2011 through 2014.

The economy of big data industries will be revolutionized by SAP HANA in-memory technology on several industry platforms. An International Data Corporation (IDC)) research report indicates that the global marketplace is moving towards *Intelligent Economy*. This will enable business analytics with a big data tool with in-memory technology. In-memory technology retrieves the data faster, which will improve financial supply chain, customer relationship, and supplier relationship management processes. Following is a discussion of the implication of big data in business, industry, and government decision-making.

Convergence and Decision-Making Processes

The global marketplace is gearing towards convergence. The rise of technological convergence requires big data appliance distribution and full integration with SAP business applications for decision-making frameworks. Olofson predicted that data will need to power up organizations to shift gears to products and supply chain improvements in specific business regions. Bulking up of Business Intelligence will be entirely fueled by big data.

The IDC conducted a study about big data and SAP analytics to augment the decision-making processes, insight enhancement, and ultra-blazing speed of data processing in organizations. The distribution of big data analytics for processing large volumes of data sets leads to the creation of new opportunities for decision-making at all levels of an organization. Olofson found the IDC has a tool called IDC's Decision-Making Frame of Reference, designed to meld decision types with risk management analysis. Thus, every decision made from big data analytics enables automation in three types of decisions: strategic decisions, operational decisions, and tactical decisions.

The IDC in 2012 conducted a customer survey to find out which tools they are leveraging to support the decision management framework in their organizations. The survey included both Information Technology and business. One of the basic problems found during the survey was that customers were unable to determine the data needed to enable the decision management framework. In some cases, the organizations were contemplating getting new data sources, or adding more data to the existing databases that would lead to quality decision-making. Most of the customers were of the opinion that the cost of their hardware configuration and software upgrades could lead to budget creep, which could be very high. The customers also did not perceive a push in business due to their lack of awareness of big data analytics and the advantages it can provide.

The organizations in the survey needed to see the business value and low hardware and software costs needed to leverage the new big data analytics. For example, IBM DB2 BLU 10.5 provides free complementary upgrades to the existing SAP customers with IBM DB2 database application specific licensing. The organizations want near real-time results with big data appliances. The culture of an organization leads to the choice of software and hardware for big data analytics, and as such, they are looking for the business value in terms of the capital investment, with zero footprint architecture that would decrease the footprint of their existing software and hardware. Olofson argued Organizations need elimination of manual operations and introduce process automation, decision automation, integration with their supply planning, and enterprise resource planning systems. Big data analytics should bring maturity in the way business is conducted. The following discussion is a survey of the two classes of data that must be accommodated in any new innovation pertaining to the management of big data.

Classes of Data

The IDC has categorized big data technology appliances into two different classes: hot data or big data in motion, and cold data or big data at rest. The big data in motion can be defined as accelerated, surging, alpine-volumes of data that requires action after the arrival, for example, stock exchange data, or the remote frequency identifier (RFID) for warehouse management operations.

In case of big data in motion use cases, a master data governance strategy is defined for filtering out the dirty data, and receiving standardized data in decipherable and homogeneous formats. Such filtering is applied in multiple layers. In this case, the filtering is done by the big data receiving application. This requires a complicated event information-processing engine for extracting the new data against the sustained data in the system from the in-memory cache.

The big data at rest, or cold data, requires the technological transformational capabilities to (a) gather the data instantly at the point of arrival; (b) bring order to the chaotic data; (c) transform the data, and; (d) perform analysis. This keeps the data in a storage place for text analytics, predictive analytics, and data mining processes. Recently, the IDC indicated that unstructured data does not really mean that the data has no structure. Unstructured data means a data type and format that cannot be interpreted intelligently by some specific programs or schemas in the existing data warehousing systems. In the case of structured data, the schema manager controls the data structure. If the schema manager does not manage the structured data it should be intelligently interpreted in a readable format by the program code. In the case of unstructured data, the data has a specific format and type, for example, extensible markup language (XML). The data resides in page headers, enclosed inside the tags, and is not easily read by the program if not already designed in that way. A major concern to the management of big data is the massive explosion of all forms of media distribution, as discussed in the following section.

Big data in Media Distribution

The big data universe is beginning to explode and to accelerate a faster change in the media industry as well. The percentage of

Internet usage from 2001 to 2012 has grown from 5% to 12%. The radio economy has dwindled down slightly from 43% to 33% due to growth in the television economy. The television digital industry revolution has sustained the momentum-of-growth rate from 45% to 44%. The usage of reading news via Internet, mobile, and various other social media sites, has reduced the consumption of newspapers in the publishing industry from 7% to 5%.

The advertising revenues from television and radio have risen twice from 2001 to 2012. The global population has switched the consumption from the conventional integration points to digital media applications. The digital revolution has turned media consumption into a planet of applications. The information explosion on mobile devices for social media, product shopping, consumerization of data over the smart phones, consumerization of video online and mobile have all had a significant influence on the media sector of the industry as well. For example, in Europe, digital video traffic is expected to grow from 2,200 PB (Petabytes) during 2011 to 11,400 PB 2016. Digital media video advertising will grow from 660 PB during 2011 to 2,500 PB in 2016.

The US is leading the content explosion globally. Europe is matching the US on the consumerization of over-the-top content (OTT). The penetration rate of US on the OTT is currently at 32%. Europe's OTT rate is anywhere between 20% to 29%. In four years from 2009 to 2012 data has grown from 6% to 20%. The growth of media audio, video over PCs, mobiles, and tablets has been indelible. Data consumerization on mobile devices has increased 5 times between 2008 and 2013.

Digital video disc (DVD) and Blu-ray economies are on the decline. Consumers are embracing the new digital media revolution by streaming video from Amazon Instant Video and Netflix streaming services, iTunes movies, Google Play movies, and Hulu Plus. The direct digital delivery distribution of video and audio content has shut down major storefronts such as Blockbuster. The big data of streaming audio and video has overtaken traditional Blu-ray and DVD discs. Sales revenue of $18 billion dollars on DVD and Blu-ray discs was reported as of 2012. Cloud computing, the ability to move the data from one storage device to another, has been a catalyst for the business transformation of digital media revolution.

In 2013, DVD and Blu-ray physical discs consumerization decreased again. The ability to rent a movie and stream it rather than buy it has exploded digital sales for Apple, Amazon instant video, Wal-Mart's Vudu, and Hulu Plus. It is in this arena where big data analytics can provide suggestions for viewing or listening to a myriad of offerings. Big data analytics can suggest streaming the big data and can understand and analyze customer trends to make the video or audio instantly available, which will boost sales revenues.

The digital revolution combined with groundbreaking technologies is changing the face of conventional television networks. The surge in the technologies has created a new wave of expansion in the digital industry. The surge has allowed owners to transmit their content with big data analytics at lightning speed on the Internet without going through the content aggregators, distributors such as cable television, or satellite operators. Big data analytics brings a lean approach to content broadcast through the Google fiber-optic network and Verizon fiber optic service (FiOS) as well as regular broadband services. Enterprises that can access the digital revolution enabled by big data streaming can tap into revenues from the $10 billion the industry has created. Kelly[12] reported that Experimental Google Fiber Television in Kansas City has launched more than 160 channels streaming at one gigabit per second (1 Gbps).

Netflix operates Amazon Web Services, a big data cloud computing platform. Big data algorithms maintain high availability with high-end Intel Xenon E5 processors to stream their movies to 40 countries. Netflix historically had Oracle RDBMS as their backend database in 2007. However, Netflix has shifted the paradigm to the NoSQL big data movement. Netflix replaced Oracle RDBMS with Apache Cassandra in 2008. This is an example of how big data can enhance the media industry streaming movies. This also increased the disaster recovery mechanism for Netflix from a single point failure of central Oracle RDBMS to something very sophisticated and distributed on big data platform. The Anytime database scheme required design revisions. Netflix required downtime with Oracle RDBMS.

Apache Cassandra revolutionized the video-on-demand (VOD) big data analytics for Netflix, particularly when run on the virtualization of hardware. The initial move to Amazon's SimpleDB big data did not yield high scalability for Netflix. Integrating Netflix with Apache Cassandra never requires changes to their schema, hence, requires no downtime. Apache Cassandra stores entire Netflix movie metadata, customer reviews, customer profile data, generated logs, and bookmarks for an instant watch queue. Netflix also maintains the data on the multi-node cluster architecture of Apache Cassandra to halt multiple points of failures. Some pieces of data may be down on the distributed cluster data centers, but not as a whole since it performs on 50 Cassandra clusters with some 750 nodes. Netflix processes more than 50,000 reads for every second, and 100,000 writes for every second. Per day, on average, 2.1 billion reads are processed by Cassandra on Netflix, and 4.3 billion writes in a day.

Netflix constructed its patent tool Genie to run on distributed Hadoop clusters on Amazon Elastic MapReduce as an application

programming interface (API) service. Amazon offers Hadoop infrastructure platform-as-a-service with Amazon Elastic MapReduce
(EMR) to manage Netflix big data workload jobs and resource
management. Amazon supports the Apache Hadoop distribution
file system via EMR. As well, Bootstrap action is a mechanism
that allows configuring the nodes of the cluster by running a script
stored from Amazon S3 on EMR. Amazon EMR allows running
queries from Apache Hive as well with Hive QL language script.
Netflix stores the data on Apache Cassandra for flexibility and to
implement the security mechanism. Finally, Apache Cassandra
allows robust internal security authorizations. Another solution to
the management of big data is Hadoop and DB2, as discussed in
the following section.

Apache Hadoop integration with SAP HANA

Apache Hadoop is an open-source distribution from Apache licensing foundation. Apache Hadoop is written in Java language operating
on earlier Google MapReduce framework model. Apache Hadoop
can process colossal volumes of datasets with a distributed cluster
technology by spreading the data blocks from multiple nodes. This
technology performs database mining techniques, database indexing, and analysis of the logs. The architecture of Hadoop distribution sits on the Hadoop distributed file system (HDFS) that extends
the data across multiple nodes. The built-in Hadoop MapReduce
engine breaks down the tasks and workloads and spreads them across
several nodes for parallel processing.

Big data tools in the market provide real-time data analytics for
actionable intelligence to the organizations. Sometimes, data not
retrieved or represented in a fraction of a second can make a difference in a decision management framework. The big data mainstream
industries such as finance, government, retail, manufacturing, and

healthcare require mountains of data from various data sources as well as the ability to store this data on a highly scalable and elastic database platform. Once the data is stored, the real-time analytics platform requires blazing speed retrieval and decomposition of the data to perform the analysis. The real-time data analytics platform should provide robust security authorizations, and integration across enterprise resource planning systems such as SAP while retaining high performance. SAP HANA has partnered an alliance with Intel distribution for Apache Hadoop platform.

The security authorization for big data is of paramount importance for manageability and enterprise authentication. Earlier industries were skeptical about installing the Apache Hadoop platform in their production environment due to a lack of built-in robust security authorization from Apache Hadoop. Currently, however, Intel distribution with the Apache Hadoop platform for SAP HANA provides robust security to enterprises with hot data at rest and cold data in motion with cryptographic functions for seamless production deployment.

IBM DB2 Blu acceleration solution was not an enterprise-ready stack. SAP HANA single solution enables with Intel distribution of Apache Hadoop, which overcomes this problem and provides a high integration, enterprise-ready stack solution, large volume retrieval of datasets, handling structured, and unstructured data. Intel distribution on SAP HANA provides excellent security with encryption and decryption features to support data on enterprise production environments.

SAP BusinessObjects and SAP Data services powered by SAP HANA with Intel distribution provides a holistic combination for organization to soar above the competition. SAP HANA real-time data analytics software solution running on Intel Xeon E7 processors is connected to Intel Manager for Apache Hadoop distribution with SAP Smart Data Access connector for tighter integration, security, and manageability. This has eliminated the problem of retrieving unstructured big data, which is not possible without Intel distribution with Apache Hadoop platform. According to the TeraSoft performance benchmark, Intel distribution for Hadoop has proven to be up to 2.6 times faster than any other open-source distribution available in the marketplace. The 10 Gb/s Ethernet network and Intel SSD (storage and Intel Xeon processors) made this possible.

Intel Manager built for Apache Hadoop distribution facilitates easier management of configurations, accelerated deployment, and continuous monitoring of Apache Hadoop distribution. The distributed cluster-based architecture enables addition of nodes for storing the database to near-unlimited capacity rather than adding up additional costly database servers. SAP provides full support for Intel distribution of Apache Hadoop software for SAP BW, business intelligence (BI), and data services powered by HANA.

SAP HANA, as part of big data strategy, released Smart Data Access technology to build a federated query language . Smart Data Access can connect to several heterogeneous databases such as Sybase IQ, Sybase ASE, Hadoop, and Teradata. The primary use of enabling the mix of several cold data sources into HANA is to leverage the application function library (AFL) of HANA and text predictive analytics library (PAL). With this innovation, the remote data source can work as well as a local database. The homogenous query syntax from HANA can tap into heterogeneous database sources with no additional syntax conversion requirement. Customers can now store their cold data into Sybase intellectual quotient (IQ) and hot data in SAP HANA directly. With Smart Data Access and Hive, customers can access big data quickly with Intel distribution for Apache Hadoop on SAP HANA. SAP in future is aiming to support connections to Oracle and MS SQL databases as part of their Smart Data Access technology for SAP HANA.

The Role of IBM DB2 Blu Acceleration

On the other hand, IBM DB2 Blu acceleration 10.5 is rapidly evolving to include customers in the new big data and analytics market. There have been several internal benchmarks about IBM DB2 Blu within IBM and SAP HANA from SAP, and customers are unable to decide which technology to choose. In a recent benchmarking test, a star schema was built in SAP HANA with 14 billion rows in the fact table. The appliance for the test contained 160-cores and two terabytes of random access memory (RAM). The utilization of RAM showed up at 206 GB RAM. When aggregation of sales was implemented, it took under three seconds to cumulate all the amounts on the sales for billions of rows. That means roughly 2000 queries can be performed every hour for a similar number of rows. SAP HANA, unlike IBM DB2 Blu, is enterprise-ready with high availability, fault tolerance with active-active, active-passive, in-memory, and on-disk with any synchronous or asynchronous replications, or with storage replication. SAP HANA comes with one of the best disaster recovery mechanisms, and general back up and recovery procedures.

A number of big data analytics databases require compressing and decompressing the data during query execution. IBM DB2 Blu claims it comes with Actionable Compression and does not require decompression; thus, it can speed up the query to 10 times faster than its competitors. SAP HANA has to decompress the data at the time of query execution. However, on analytics views HANA does not require decompression for COUNTS.

SAP HANA supports the Intel Xeon E7s. Intel introduced the E3, E5 Xeon processors on Ivy Bridge. Intel E7 is constructed with Westmere. SAP HANA supports the E7 processor with 80 cores in contrast to E5 that supports 32 and E3 that supports eight cores. The E7 8870-V2 can support up to 240 cores and 12 TB of RAM. SAP HANA only supports running it on the hardware that is certified by SAP; it cannot allow integration or running on hardware that is not certified by SAP.

IBM heralds IBM Blu acceleration does not require any proprietary hardware; however, SAP HANA does. SAP HANA published their hardware configuration in alliance with all partners in the market to show that SAP HANA can run on any hardware configuration. On December 3, 2013, SAP has officially certified the IBM DB2 10.5 Blu acceleration solution that can work with SAP NetWeaver BW. Customers on earlier IBM DB2 versions need to upgrade to DB2 10.5 with no upgrade to SAP hardware. It can reduce the existing table size by 10 times.

SAP has also released the online service system (OSS) note 1825340 to migrate existing facts and dimension tables, Infocubes, and BW temporary tables for Linux, Unix, and Windows system platforms. However, the support related to operational data store (ODS) tables is not mentioned. Customers can now reap the benefits of BLU columnar tables. SAP customers with IBM DB2 BLU database with existing application specific licensing (ASL) can get it at no additional price to augment their SAP NetWeaver BW platforms.

Blu table is an innovative technology that results in unparalleled table storage reduction. No indexes require creation. Blu table is a column-organized table. In a conventional RDBMS, a row-based table is created with a primary index, and secondary index, if needed. The data in row-organized stores on a single volume. The Blu table data in each column is stored on a separate volume of the database. Each volume is a page on the disk. When a query fires on a column-organized table, the disk input and output operation is drastically reduced because only the columns that are queried are accessed, not all records on the Blu table. Thus, only the pages on the disk for the columns accessed are loaded onto the *in-memory*. Blu uses actionable compression technology; the data in the Blu table is highly compressed with an IBM industrial algorithm. IBM has a benchmark of improving the speed of the query and data delivery by 10 to 50 times, and compression improvement by three times to 10 times. Blu engine processes the data from Blu table with simultaneous single instruction, multiple data (SIMD) instructions.

The actionable compression in Blu engages columnar-dictionary compression by leveraging different compressed code sizes per column. It is similar to a frequency-dictionary algorithm. The most frequently used values are assigned with smaller codes while the less frequently assigned values are assigned with larger codes. For example, records contain company codes in SAP. The frequency dictionary that contains the most frequently used company codes maybe allocated with a partition size of one bit. The next 10 most frequently occurring company codes will be allocated a three-bit comprised code. The most frequent company codes, in this case, would have the highest compression of 16 times. The Blu table analyzes the sample SQL insert statements and builds histograms, allowing the compression optimizer to determine a way to maximize the compression on the most frequent occurring values. The columns of Blu table store on column groups, and each column is allocated to a column group. The column data store in fixed-size pages on the disk. An extent contains a fixed number of pages for the Blu table. The projection of the row on each column group is called a *tuplet*.

Apart from the column-level compression, a page level compression is performed. For every column-organized table, a synopsis table is created internally. This enables page skipping for scan-time savings. Unlike other in-memory solutions, Blu performs a query on compressed data without having to decompress the data during the query execution. Each query is part of the plan of tree operation and prompts the evaluation operator to load the values either into the memory or perform a specific arithmetic operation. This enables significant vector processing. The Blu column-organized tables provide a significant boost for star schema data marts for query performance.

SAP HANA database compression technology

SAP HANA has memory management for compression, memory partitioning of the columns, storage of columns, and insert only on delta mechanism. Regardless of the SQL query triggered to SAP HANA database, SAP HANA only performs *insertion on the delta* memory area of SAP HANA database. SAP HANA has powerful and robust locking mechanism and creates two separate areas for existing database and delta areas. Such locking mechanism and memory partitioning strategy are to shield the database from power outages or any disasters that can occur to the traditional or cloud-based data centers. Database operations such as DELETE and UPDATE also trigger INSERT operations to the main memory area with the record marked for DELETE and UPDATE operation. The merge mechanism at the database level will sweep through the delta area continuously to find the entries and merge with the database while SAP HANA locking mechanism monitors the entries on any open transactions conflicting with the latest UPDATE and DELETE operations. This combination secures high-speed database updates for high-velocity transactions with 100% accuracy.

The columnar storage in contiguous locations ensures high-compression of the database. SAP HANA provides such default-compression at dictionary level whenever columnar-tables get created, or row-based tables get converted to columnar-tables. The dictionary compression applies to both main and delta areas. The contiguous locations of memory in SAP HANA ensure to store the columns in consecutive memory locations for easier access to data. This database strategy primarily focuses on the reduction of cost of storage and infrastructure and provide (Database as a service) DBaaS option through SAP HANA Cloud Platform for economies of scale.

SAP HANA also offers a bevy of other compression techniques at the database for higher compression of the column stores. These compression techniques categorize advanced compression techniques. Such sophisticated compression techniques include SAP HANA prefix encoding, sparse encoding, cluster encoding, indirect encoding, and run-length encoding (RLE). Cluster encoding is highly beneficial to sort text-based values. Cluster encoding runs a search for numerous instances of identical strings by distributing the values into 1024 elements and creates an index on another column that represents the column with values. Run-length encoding classifies identical values in the column by applying the sort technique. With memory partitioning technique, SAP HANA creates another column for each column to display the count of repetitions of each string element in the column. When a query is triggered based on the value specified in the query, it would be easier to construct the retrieval of the data from the main memory based on run-length encoding. Prefix encoding stores the identical values only a single time at the top of the array with another column that samples the occurrences of each value. Indirect encoding similar to cluster encoding distributes the range of values into multiple groups of 1024 elements. Each group sweeps the unique data elements and constructs a dictionary to represent the repetition of occurrences of the data values. Sparse coding compression technique identifies the values that repeat that have higher value and eliminates those entries from the array and highlights the removed and isolated location of values.

Apache Hadoop encompasses MapReduce as the programming model for handling large volumes of data. Each data node in Apache Hadoop is a server by itself in Hadoop cluster server distributed technology. The servers are cost efficient and performance efficient at the same time. Apache Hadoop breaks down the data into multiple chunks so that concurrent data jobs can run simultaneously on multiple data nodes and servers for extreme scalability and speed. As the data increases, more data nodes can be added periodically based on the Exabyte volume growth estimates. Apache Hadoop provides fault tolerance by cloning the data running on one data node into another data node to avoid any information loss.

The strategic framework allows the MapReduce programming model to perform two steps. First, it maps the solution to multiple data chunks providing fragmentary results during the map phase. Second, the Reduce phase will assemble the scattered fragmentary results by producing the concluding solution with parallelism. The architecture of Apache Hadoop sits on top of HDFS that can store files in JavaScript Object Notation (JSON) or any native Linux operating system format. The HDFS breaks the file into multiple blocks based on the size of the blocks defined on the system. The system examines the size of the configurable block and splits the file into multiple blocks with equal sizes.

As part of the Hadoop ecosystem, there are several features to capture, store, retrieve, and distribute the data. HBase a NoSQL language provides multiple APIs that allow the storage, and retrieval of data blocks stored on the HDFS. Hive is a read-only NoSQL to read the data from the HDFS. Apache Mahout provides high scalability, and statistical calculation engine, analytic engine on top of Apache Hadoop platform. Pig Latin or simply Pig is another procedural language that can produce MapReduce programs for performing data analytics. Sqoop migrates and transfers the data between

Hadoop and traditional data marts, RDBMS. To handle the challenges of big data, a big data tool is expected to handle all the *4VS* (velocity, volume, variety, and veracity), which will be discussed in a following section. Apache Hadoop, as a big data tool, supports the *4VS* to wring the value from the big data.

Hadoop processes immense data volume with HDFS. The traditional RDBMS performs heavy validation checks on the data before it is inserted, updated, or deleted from the database storage. To perform the validations, the table needs to verify multiple tables for cross-reference and integrity. Creation of primary and secondary indexes adds heavy disk (input and output) operations. The traditional RDBMS goes through acid, consistent, isolated, durable (ACID) compliance adding extreme overhead to the CPU, as well as disk input and output operations. Apache Hadoop avoids all these overheads by boosting the data velocity. Apache Hadoop is flexible for handling data variety with a number of file formats, and directly dumps the files into a Linux operating system without mandating a predefined file format. The fourth data veracity could be a double-edged sword as it deals with the quality of the data by eliminating the dirty data. SAP data services with information stewardship can provide a quality solution for filtering out the dirty data on top of Apache Hadoop.

The data clusters from different sources. The dirty data can be profiled, analyzed, and monitored with Information Steward on top of SAP data services powered by SAP HANA. The categorization of data and standardization of data must conform to the master data governance strategy. A cleansing package builder can generate the classification of data. It cleanses the dirty data with merge, purge, consolidation, and matching techniques of SAP Business Objects Information Steward data services on top of SAP HANA.

In terms of storage of data, Apache Hadoop differs from SAP HANA. Hadoop stores any variety file on the disk while SAP HANA stores the data in-memory. The conventional RDBMS SAP HANA stores structured data in a predefined schema format. Hadoop is schema-less. In terms of data velocity, in-memory is faster than another type of database. An enterprise getting data from multiple data sources are integrated with SAP. External to SAP it requires an elastic data store to capture different formats of the files. This is where Apache Hadoop can capture, store, and process the data through SAP HANA.

Data mining techniques, calculations, and analytics run from Hadoop. In an organization, Hadoop can store the data flowing in the form of various formats. These formats could be media files, social networking platforms at raw data level, emails, documents, transactional data from externally sourced systems or online shopping carts, and customer surveys at granularity level with web server logs. SAP HANA is integrated with Apache Hadoop, hence, can pull the data stored in Hadoop into SAP HANA for performing aggregations and create OLAP fact tables to export to SAP HANA.

The Four V's

A research project was conducted by IDC on behalf of SAP to determine answers to questions related to the disentanglement of OLAP and OLTP. Results of a survey involved 759 participants spanning the globe. Information technology managers and business managers responsible for blending transactional applications and analytical applications to make a decision were polled.

Few participants had myths about big data appliances. The participants in the survey believed that big data means processing gargantuan volumes of data with Apache Hadoop distribution. Few believed it was a single corporate-wide requirement for building and addressing an indistinguishable and homologous requirement. Forty percent of the participants believed that big data was only a concern for those organizations with a large volume of data sets. Twenty-six percent of the participants believed that the data variation had to be monumental to represent the variety of the data. Twenty-four percent believed big data included media companies and had to deal with near real-time streaming data or streaming data analytics. In addition, other 10% believed that it had to do with those organizations that require high performance in the throughput. Participants did not consider big data as an element of delivering business value, of any decision management framework, or of purification of data. IDC has defined big data as a next generation technology, and that design architectonics infuse value from the dawn of the intelligent economy to massively larger data sets for analysis and delivery, differentiated by *four Vs*. A discussion of the Four Vs follows.

Volume. The volume does not necessarily indicate processing gargantuan volumes of data. A few may have data stored in terabytes, or for that matter, even in gigabytes, in contrast to the exabytes of data extracted from the social media networking. Big data has some complex processing calculations for arriving at the reports for analysis and decision management framework.

Variety. The aggregation of data from multiple sources in a variety of data formats can be evaluated to see the data tunneling through the application and retained as big data. Big data applications frequently fuse the data from a variety of data connections (commonly both in-house data formats such as SAP standardized formats and exterior formats outside the organization that are, for example, non SAP formats). It also deals with data of distinctly different types (well-regulated, or unregulated data types). This is business-critical universe for both technological and lurking ramification. Fusing data types is a convoluted realm for business.

Velocity. Speed of thought analysis and elasticity of the data constantly moving through the organization depends on the number of job workloads sprawl on the distributed cluster nodes. The velocity of the data is purely dependent on requirements of business processes in the organization.

Value. Ultimately, in the context of big data, value refers to (a) the early hours of the rise of the intelligent economy; (b) the important steps of embarking on a journey of disbursement of the money spent on the technology for information processing, and; (c) the business value acquired from the adoption of big data. The advantages of adopting big data can be categorized as a strategic cutback in the total software, hardware, and infrastructure, all of which are capital investments of the company. The result of a transformation to a new era of in-memory computing, the organization will experience (a) improved serviceable and operational competencies in the organization; (b) unravelment of complex calculations, and; (c) elimination of drudgery of manual IT operations. Big data is a way of bulking up business intelligence and instilling new competitive advantage to create growth opportunitie. Big data employs the newest and most powerful methods for manageability, integration with enterprise, supply chain, and customer relationship management systems.

Critique of Previous Scholarly Research

Gartner research provided key challenges faced by current customers that are leveraging SAP BW. The lack of in-memory technology was cited as an increasingly complex problem in systems on December 27, 2012. SAP HANA can simplify the data modeling in SAP BW that combines several tables and solves columnar database storage. SAP BW powered by HANA can remain as a central core solution for existing SAP BW customers to move to the in-memory technology solution for extraction, transformation, loading and reporting the data for analytics purposes. A significant HANA assessment and feasibility study needs to be conducted to analyze the existing data modeling and highlight the benefits to achievement of goals with SAP HANA implementation. The clients can leverage a 100% discount of BWA solution with a SAP HANA purchase.

SAP released SAP BW powered by HANA in 2012. SAP HANA had proved to be 3,600 times faster than traditional RDBMS databases when SAP BW deployed with Oracle, MSSQL, and DB2 database servers. SAP recently conducted a HANA test in the construction industry on their SAP NetWeaver platform of Business suite, and concluded that the SAP HANA 1.0 in-memory computing technology ran 3,600 times faster than the queries performed on traditional RDBMS to retrieve the customer data of business transactions. The infrastructure used for setting up SAP HANA was an eight-core server. It was running at 2.27 GHz speed, a minimum of half TB of main memory, two TB of solid-state drive with an unbiased open source software operating system. Despite the groundbreaking developments of SAP HANA, the calculations performed on SAP BI Universe still need to be pushed down to SAP HANA to boost the performance of the universe reporting. The following two sections summarize the findings of the review of literature with the objectives of the present study.

Inferences for the Present Study

In Chapter 1, a summary of the SAP HANA conceptual framework was provided. This framework has shown that SAP HANA is a pioneering in-memory database-computing platform. Chapter

1 contained data that indicated SAP HANA can outmaneuver various in-memory database platforms that are in the market, primarily for performance benchmarks, atomicity, and the ability to handle huge dataset calculations with the algorithms to provide predictive analytics. SAP HANA handles the database volumes with DRAM. However, futuristic flash memory has proven cost-effective for databases such as Aerospike.

Conceptual Framework for Present Study

Globally, organizations are entering digital petabyte age for consumerization of data enabled for decision-making. Professor Sang Kyun Cha from Seoul National University constructed the first-generation in-memory columnar database P*TIME IMDB in 2002. He launched the company Transact In-Memory Inc. for a future technology that did not exist until years later, but was subsequently was acquired by SAP in 2005. Transact in-memory Inc. was transformed later into SAP Labs Korea by 2008, which led to the third-generation in-memory database SAP HANA.

Customers want to access data at a blazing speed and process data blocks even faster than traditional disk-based RDBMS systems to make timely informed decisions. The information explosion on data volume has to be in real-time and in-memory; the faster the business reacts to the data they see, the quicker they are in a position to make decisions. The volume of data comes in massive amounts in unstructured and structured patterns; thus, enterprises are today facing a bigger corporate conundrum than has existed previously.

Organizations want to manage the information coming from logistics, financial planning, materials management, CRM, SRM, SCM, and IT departments. Processing data in a timely fashion that can be broken down into smaller segments of organized data and converted into analyzable datamart scenarios that can finally lead to decision-making is the objective of all data management. For instance, SAPA HANA leverages a tool, SAP HANA studio, to integrate all IT systems. SAP HANA studio dynamically extracts the flattened data from the dimensions of SAP HANA views. SAP HANA can transform it into the target systems of SAP ERP, SCM, CRM, SRM, and PLM. SAP HANA studio can enable integration with other systems by rendering the environment for development, administration, and data provisioning. SAP HANA studio was built as a Java-based application on Eclipse platform; thus, an Eclipse-based environment provides an open, integrated development environment for development of data content with a variety of applications and tools.

SAP HANA studio running on Eclipse platform works on a local file based system. Once SAP HANA studio activates these design object files, those will be bound to a run time repository of SAP HANA as a catalog tree in a custom-specific schema. The catalog tree mirrors the metadata of the database structure. SAP HANA studio has several perspectives to view such as an administration console perspective to administer and monitor the SAP HANA system. The modeler perspective can build the reporting models. These models developed for storing information can be further broken down into specific views such as calculation views with calculated values, analytic views, and attribute views with analytical privileges.

Unlike the earlier SAP BW version of a dimension that is tied to, a single model attribute view in SAP HANA can be as an object with polymorphic attributes. The attribute view leverages any other business purposes requiring accessing the same database views for a different objective. The usage of attribute views is not limited to building a data model, but can be reused by calculation views and analytical views as appropriate. Ideally, the purpose behind building the attribute views is to store the master data attributes; however, it can be built to model the transactional data attributes as well.

SAP HANA studio allows building analytic views that are similar to InfoCubes in SAP NetWeaver BW. The analytic view can contain any number of dimensions and data arrays of attributes. In the traditional database model of SAP NetWeaver BW, the data is always stored through a process called extract, transform, and load (ETL). This requires several steps to perform to store the transformed data into the physical tables; this increases the number of processes and makes the processing speed slower. This is where SAP HANA analytic view is beneficial as it first builds a plan and a schema for transformation of data to store in the database tables. This roadmap for transformation of data allows the data to be transformed dynamically at runtime without going through the intensive processes. Unlike the classical database table, the dimensions stored in the analytic view are not planned. The data flattening will occur from the analytic view by grouping all the data from the dimensions. The flattening occurs based on the extraction from a required system. It is driven by the requirement from the online analytical processing (OLAP) cube of analytic view. It is used for the average of the inventory price, total of the quantities in a month.

The SAP HANA analytic view stores the data in a star schema by configuring the number of dimension tables in a star sequence design connecting to the fact table. The data in SAP HANA star schema remains flattened out. Data loads have shown speeds times faster than the traditional star schema based SAP NetWeaver BW Infocubes with star schema.

Calculation views in SAP HANA are similar to the multiprovider concept in earlier SAP NetWeaver BW with which to provide the calculations representing graphical view, and with the SQL script calculation view. The SQL statements can be written within the calculation view to perform any calculations with numerous fact tables. The SQL written in SAP patent version is called SQL script programming language. Calculation views are developed to solve the complex business conundrums by joining the attribute views and analytical views to provide a reporting capability either in graphical format or SQL script calculation view.

SAP integrates with multiple systems such as ERP, SCM, CRM, SRM, PLM, and financial supply chain management (FSCM). In addition to integration, data loads, replication, and transformation of the flattened structures with multiple systems, SAP HANA also gears for the integration with Apache Hadoop to solve big data business problems. In today's world, open source software vendors are building solutions to deal with massive amounts of big data volume. Apostles of the NoSQL movement evolved as an alternative solution to SQL-based products. SQL-based products are not able to provide a high availability or the scalability needed for lightning speed or computations and transformation of the data into the required system based on the business requirements.

Organizations are tapping into the big data market globally. It is estimated to grow more than 25% from 2013 to 2018 with projected revenues of $46+ billion dollars. Financial, evolving technology sectors, electronics, high tech, media, broadcasting, communications, holiday business, and service sector started leveraging the big data platforms quickly. The adoption is intended to analyze the consumer trends to build a new product or to improve an already launched product. SAP HANA with all its attributes, analytical, and calculation views can build the structured data aka *hot data* that can retrieve from *in-memory*. Apache Hadoop, when connected to SAP HANA, can process data in petabytes.

Big data comes in human-organized and unstructured patterns that have been generated by organizations over historical periods. Traditional relational databases are not spry enough to handle the volume of data due to its sheer size and volume and velocity at which it is generated. Organizations analyze and understand consumer trends. They look at the isochronous configurations of data based on their store purchases and online electronic purchase transactions providing the insights on consumer behavior and the drivers for making decisions to purchase. Gartner Inc. has defined big data with four characteristics of data information: Volume, Velocity, Variety, and Veracity as defined in the following paragraphs.

- Volume: The volume of big data for giant organizations usually begins with petabytes (10^{15} bytes). It goes all the way up to Exabyte (10^{18} bytes), zettabyte (10^{21} bytes), and yottabyte (10^{24} bytes, i.e., 1,000,000,000,000,000,000,000,000 bytes). The general relational database tools can handle up to 10 terabytes (10^{12} bytes). According to IDC research, the world has generated over 1.8 zettabytes of data in 2011 alone. This was fueled by more than 5 billion phones, 30 billion pieces of shared data on Facebook, 20 billion internet searches, shipping containers logistics, retail packaging and energy meter censors.

- Velocity: The big data can travel at unprecedented rates clocking in at an average velocity of 5 TB per second (now that is 5,000 gigabytes per second). The big data travels on an accelerated and hyper connected content delivery framework and social media networks. The big data is also the data populated from climate sensors, censor data, RFID, and global positioning system (GPS). Stock exchange buy and sell trade-in transactions within 100 microseconds.

- Variety: The rising flood of the big data can come in with high-speed velocity (in and out). The elasticity of data comes in several flavors. It comes in with combinations of unstructured data such as photos, messages, and videos. Several other forms that can be processed with database tools such as NoSQL can store data without the SQL itself on software products such as Google Dremel, Tokyo Cabinet, CouchDB, Redis, MongoDB, Talend, and Apache Cassandra. The reason for not having SQL is to avoid indexes and databases. Database relationship technology called Dremel can crunch one trillion pieces of data with a single click. Dremel provides marketing research data under 30 seconds to Google to make product intelligent decisions either by launching a new product or improving an existing product. Google coined this term as *Google Zeitgeist* to synthesize the aggregated content from billions of search queries Google receives every day. SAP HANA is a big data solution for large organizations to analyze the data for corporate level decisions.

- Veracity: The elasticity of the data can show some disposition in terms of the quality and patterns that contain noise, anomaly from the regular data models. It is important to store the data that is hypercritical to the fully functioning business units of the organization that helps the database tool to build a mining technique to extract the data with blazing performance.

In an *Intelligent Economy* organizations require data for *Actionable Intelligence*, hence the quality of the data is of paramount importance. The quality of data can determine the decision outcomes. Dirty data is defined as data that is inadequate, inaccurate, redundant, and duplicated in the organization over the years that either requires merge or purge techniques. When an organization sets quarterly targets for their departments based on the data in the organization, it is important to have refined data to achieve the targets. Recent research conducted by the research firm insiderRESEARCH, and Gartner that stated 67% of the SAP based companies gave the feedback about dirty data that spread across multiple systems and applications. SAP based companies (64%), stated that dirty data gets clogged in the system when there are multiple versions of the truth, and it could be either source or the destination.

(25%) that run SAP are unable to make decisions due to the quality of the data. Research also states that by 2015 the majority of these will have a Chief Data Officer (CDO) position. The dirty data stored historically in the database for the organization can clog database mining and can easily turn into a bottleneck to database mining from the big data. As part of Veracity, it is important to have a database management strategy. This strategy can help to define the database quality levels when storing the information in the database, which helps to filter through various data attributes in the system that are not really needed for the business functionality from day one. Organizations that analyze the data at the speed of light can enter the fray with competitors. Some of the historical data might even have lost relevance. Analyzing data with the current trends of the data patterns can give a competitive edge to firms. It is apposite to archive the historical data for auditing purposes.

Table 1

Global Online Population by Country 2012

Country	Online Population	Percentage
North America	272,066.000	78.90%
Latin America	215,939.400	37.74%
Europe	476,213,933	64.50%
Asia	922,329,554	22.14%
Africa	118,609,620	11.60%
Oceania	21,293,830	58.19%

Source: White, 2012.

Review of NoSQL Database Tools in the Marketplace

The big data has been making new waves of technologies in the marketplace, which has introduced a sea change in the speed and architecture of the database for data retrieval. The global population has generated much of this data from the past few years. There are more than 2.095 billion people that are 30% of world's population accessing the data online over the Internet. These people spend 35 billion hours on the Internet, which is equivalent to 3.9 million years. The average time spent by the global Internet user is around 16 hours per month, and US Internet user spend approximately 32 hours per month. The Table 1 gives the world's online population break down by each region.

Table 2

Global Online Population Activities 2012

Activity	Percentage
Online Shopping	5%
Social Networking	22%
Multi-Media sites	13%
Searches	21%
Emails and Communication	19%
Reading Content	20%

Source: White, 2012.

Table 2 shows the activities spent online that create a tremendous amount of big data for industries, organizations, and social media networking consumer trends. The global online population creates avalanche of big data. The global online population over the last two years generated 90% of world's big data. The data is massively created by the online community from the Internet either by online shopping purchases, social media networking, multi-media, and communications. These activities are riding a new wave of big data generation underpinned by the Internet and smart phones. Each minute, the world online population is generating gargantuan volumes of data. More than 684,478 pieces of content are read and shared per second on social media networks such as Facebook and Twitter. Over 200 million emails are sent each minute. The online shopping activities have a monetary value of $272,000+ per minute, roughly $391 million per day. A volume of two million search queries is performed worldwide per minute.

Google is visited by a 153.4 million global online population and has registered, on average, more than one billion search queries on Google search engine. YouTube garners more than four billion views per day. Unique visitors per month who visit Facebook number 137.6 million. Sixty hours of new content video gets uploaded to YouTube every minute. There are more than 250 million tweets generated on Twitter. Apple acquired Topsy Labs, a big data analytics company, for $200 million to analyze Twitter feeds and gear towards consumer preferences and trends.

To process extreme big data, the database has to be robust with ultra-blazing speed. The database has to be interactive with hashing techniques to chunk the data into buckets by primary key for columnar storage for high scalability and greater performance. The world needs database tools that are flexible to capture the data, store, and access with lightning speed. These database tools should analyze this data to predict the consumer trends on online shopping, social networking, tastes, traits, likes, and preferences of the global population.

The current schema of RDBMS tools are not typically designed for this gigantic volume of data. The data types defined within the architecture of RDBMS do not support extraction and storage of this extreme big league data. RDBMS was mainly designed for a structured database with specific defined data types, not meant for handling unstructured or semi-structured data types to store and retrieve. For this reason, NoSQL database tools have been released to the marketplace to support these features. These tools provide an elastic database tool that can stretch the data as the demand rises in organiaations across the globe.

The NoSQL tool has been designed to support and process massive volumes of data from the cloud, as most of the today's data is entering and residing in the cloud. The traditional RDBMS stores the data in multiple tables with defined schema joining several tables with primary and foreign key relationships. The data extraction has to be performed by linking and joining various relationships based on the data type and the cardinality of the relationship between multiple database tables. The entire data base is stored in rows and columns. Updates occurr to the database tables.

Several cascading updates need to occur based on the relationships similar to the extract process for reading the data from multiple tables. The architecture of the NoSQL database is schemaless. The NoSQL database is not dependent or requires the definition of the scheme between multiple tables. Instead, it takes various chunks of heterogenous data types. The NoSQL database synthesizes the information by aggregating it to a JavaScript Object Notation (JSON) document format that combines hundreds of tables into a single document format by storing the rows data in a column.

The advantage of having NoSQL database tool is to extract massive amounts of voluminous data with a distributed technology because the RDBMS requires scaling up the servers to extract the data from highly scalable servers. In today's business, people want to access the data *in the moment* in *real time*. Every time the data delays, fail to take action either to grab the opportunity or to mitigate an existing risk identified by the organization as part of enterprise risk management.

The NoSQL database can operate either on a virtual or a physical server with a distributed architecture technology. The servers can be added as needed as a cluster as part of distributed technology. As the people using the data increases, the number of servers can be added to the clutter to boost the performance. The central application stack of NoSQL remains unaltered. It always processes the data from a single distributed database cluster that is not impacted with the addition of new database servers to the cluster.

The addition of database servers to the distributed cluster based on the demand of the organizations also makes it a cost-effective approach to the solution, as opposed the single high scalable server approach of the RDBMS database. As the dynamic needs of the organization are predicted in the beginning, single, scalable servers are estimated to be a probabilistic memory storage number. The storate number may exceed the demand in the future, thus leading either to a database migration onto a new highly scalable server increasing the cost of the database upgrades for the organization. Thus, NoSQL database distributed technology comes with shards that store different parts of shared collection of data. It incorporates the auto sharding concept based on the demand and supply equation of the organizational business needs.

The queries written in NoSQL database do not have complex schemas to join multiple tables with various complex cardinal relationships to extract the data. The NoSQL database queries are simplistic in nature and can extract the data from a complex structured, unstructured, and semi-structure database. The data at times is cached in the memory of the database instead of always storing it in disk files. The new database in this instance is purely instantiated in the memory. In traditional RDBMS when the database query is closed, the data ceases to exist elsewhere in the memory; to retrieve the data again, a new query has to be fired making a round trip to the database engine again, thus taking extensive time to reload the data from the database server. The database is literally disconnected from the entire application stack. In case of integrated caching on the distributed technology of NoSQL database, the data is cached *in-memory* by creating an independent memory cache for the query to access the data despite if the connection to the database has been closed, thus retrieving the data at lightning blazing speed. The following are a few NoSQL tools that were available in the marketplace before SAP HANA. Taking a look at these tools provides the pros and cons of the tools in the marketplace over SAP HANA.

Google Dremel. Google built big data Analytics Dremel for *Actionable Intelligence* on the new products Google releases on the marketplace and to improve the existing products. Recently, Google launched Google BigQuery for organizations that are outside the corporate firewall of Google Inc. The concept of BigQuery relies mainly on heavy parallel processing of the query on multiple servers. The query can be fired on all Google proprietary cloud platform such as YouTube, Google Docs, Google Search engine, Google gmail. Google BigQuery is the exteriorization of Dremel by providing a public RESTful (Representational State Transfer) API. Google Dremel can crunch 35 billion rows within few seconds. The Query fires with the mechanism of parallelization on thousands of servers at the same time. Google Dremel built on big data architecture and in-memory computing with columnar database storage. For this reason, the performance throughput on the compressed database cubes is pretty high. The data in each column gets stored on a separate volume of the database, unlike the conventional relational database that stores each record on a single volume. The merits of such storage not only lead to a tightly integrated compression ration of the database, but the query will only scan the necessary columns that are part of the query. However, Dremel only supports the read operations and does not support any write and update operations to the database.

Tokyo Cabinet. Tokyo Cabinet is a NoSQL database tool written in C language. It is the next generation NoSQL database tool followed by Berkeley-DB, an ultra-blazing database tool that can extract the data. The source code of Tokyo Cabinet is made available to the general public by Sourceforge.net as free software for anyone to modify the source code and distribute it to the general public.

Tokyo Cabinet has APIs library that stores the routines and works as a dbm (database manager). The main features of Tokyo Cabinet supports the hashing techniques to build fixed size data chunks for faster data retrieval by developing a primary key for the chunk called bucket. The other modes include table mode, b-tree mode. The Tokyo Cabinet will work based on the key and the value given to the database, and retrieves the data rapidly based on the key in the search query. The entire data is hash coded using extensible hashing techniques and stored. Sometimes stored in b+ tree format that allows storing the data that appears to store in the form of a tree that has definitive terminal nodes with equivalent distance between the bases. Following are the features of Tokyo Cabinet:

- Highly compressed format of the database files thus bringing reduction of database storage concept in the database
- Ultra-blazing performance thus boosting the system efficiency in terms of the rate at which the data is traveling for retrieval
- The concept of parallelization allows to spawn multiple threads when a search query is fired to the database
- The APIs have a simplistic approach to retrieving the data as opposed to the traditional relational databases
- Secure storage of the data, the database is not vulnerable by accessing the information
- Unlike several traditional RDBMS databases that do not support the 64-bit architecture, Tokyo Cabinet does support 64-bit architecture. A Japanese social network media site called mixi uses Tokyo Cabinet.

Apache CouchDB. Apache CouchDB is another product that has made waves in joining the NoSQL movement written in Erlang. It is simplistic in nature to access via hypertext transfer protocol (HTTP) RESTful APIs. It can store the data in JSON format similar to Tokyo Cabinet, Tokyo tyrant, including the data types of hash maps with bi-directional replication capabilities. The simplicity in CouchDB lies in invoking the connectivity to the database without requiring any drivers to the browser. The Map Reduce technique is leveraged in CouchDB thus making it schemaless. The CouchDB creates version of each document. The database can significantly grow in little time. Hence, an archiving and data retention strategy is required to see how much data requires retention in the database based on the periodical frequency. The JSON objects are indexed and stored in the database. Hence, the updates to the database will require more time due to the requirement of reindexing the database. Since CouchDB leverages Map Reduce technique, the indexing is not very efficient. It is mostly leveraged for analyzing the stock exchange prices.

Redis. Redis open-source software was written in C language. It is open for modifications by the global big data development community. It operates as integrated caching in-memory computing database tool that will fire the search query with a key and value that has joined the NoSQL database movement due to surging in big data. The drawback of Redis, unlike Tokyo Cabinet, is that, it does not support parallelization of spawning multiple threads for the search query; it runs as a single thread, thus taking long time to retrieve the data. The advantage of Redis is that it takes operates in two modes of persistency of the memory. One being the snap shooting of capturing the *now* moment of the data at a timestamp, the other mode of persistence being AOF (append only file) at periodical intervals. The auto sharding is not highly capable in Redis due to lack of scalability in the application. However, distributed technology of storing data objects on multiple servers, and faster accessing supported as long as the retrieval is via snap shooting mode. It can be implemented efficiently for business applications such as CRM systems. Since it is a server by itself, it is not largely leveraged for database operations that require round trip to the servers unlike Tokyo Cabinet that has embedded data stores. Guardian.co.uk, digg, bump, Flickr from Yahoo, and twitter all use Redis.

MongoDB. MongoDB is a start-up company funded by CIA (Central Intelligence Agency) as part of their In-Q-Tel project. MongoDB written in C language is OSS (open-source software) that still has the capabilities of indexing the data stored in the database. It had the auto-sharding capabilities to break the data into buckets and chunks and processed the shared data with ultra-blazing performance. The updates are faster with MongoDB despite the indexing functionality that is available in MongoDB on the database. The most significant advantage of MongoDB is the ability to process large cubes of data volumes as well as the ability to fire dynamic queries at run time without fixed values. MondoDB is the tool the market is looking for as opposed to Apache CouchDB. MongoDB provides the capabilities of horizontal scaling by dealing with aggregation of documents defined as part of the tree structure, nodes, and sub nodes for extremely fast data access. MongoDB is schemaless similar to most of the other NoSQL tools in the marketplace for greater performance. The documents are binary hash coded and stored in BSON format (Binary JavaScript object notation). Data replication with bi-directional capabilities is available in MongoDB. The disadvantage of MongoDB is it does not have a security implementation model to protect from risks or to incorporate a security authorization concept to control the roles accessing the data. Unlike other NoSQL tools, it is not meant for supporting business intelligence systems and database warehouse solutions.

Companies such as Stripe, MetLife, SAP, MTV, Source Forge, wordnik, uberVu, and ADP run production deployment of MongoDB. Media companies implement it, such as Forbes, The New York Times, CNN, and Chicago Tribune as well.

The Unique Identification Project (UID) world's colossal massive biometrics database in India known as *Aadhaar* to capture demographic and personal information, and biometrics runs MongoDB. Talend open source software developed in Java issued under Apache free licensing. Talend, a big data open data enterprise integration platform, can connect to several big data analytics software tools including SAP HANA. Talend can be connected to SAP HANA with the configuration of server parameters, and bridging SAPJCO. jar file. Talend can perform many operations such as aggregation, harmonization of data, and data cleansing especially from massively large datasets. Talend is capable of rendering high elasticity, and scalability of data by running inside native Apache Hadoop.

The mission critical factor for Talend is data quality. On the security side, it can support Kerberos native protocol authentication for a robust environment on Hadoop distribution. Talend comes with different flavors of data platforms such as master data management (MDM) for data governance, data integration, Enterprise server beans, data quality, and big data analytics. Talend recently received funding of $40 million to push forward with their go-to-market strategy.

Apache Cassandra. Apache Cassandra is a new paradigm in the marketplace that has joined the NoSQL movement for facing new challenges of big data, written in Java language open-source software distributed by Apache. Cassandra introduced the concept of big table with features to fire the queries with commands that look similar to SQL commands, however, does not have features of inner or outer joins of traditional RDBMS system tools. Apache Cassandra is best suited for industries that have heavy data to write to the database on a daily basis, thus reducing the time for updates to the system. In conjunction with Apache Hadoop, the Map and Reduce technique can be implemented. Cassandra has been implemented in real-time many industries such as social media network platform Twitter, streaming the movie with big data Netflix.

The IMDB technologies ability to handle large volumes of data for industrial applications, and integration with enterprise resource planning systems with minimum in-memory capabilities of RAM on a distributed cluster technology were researched as part of the present study. The classical data warehouse such as SAP NetWeaver BW has a procedural sequence responsible for completing an ETL process. The organization will set up a data governance and data warehousing strategy based on which, for the specific scenario of BW, the ETL activity will be performed after evaluation of multiple data sources and targets. The extraction and transformation occur in SAP NetWeaver BW as the basic step, in case of a possible SAP source system, invoking the SAP BW API service leveraging API layer. In the case of other potential systems, where the format is non-standardized SAP format, a file interface can be leveraged. Thus, the data can be extracted into a comma separated value format. Any relational databases that require the access from SAP NetWeaver BW for the extraction process can initiate a request. The request contains Universal Data (UD) Connect. The data in the target SAP NetWeaver BW database layer is different from various sources of data that sends the data, and the transformation occurs to store the data in the format of SAP NetWeaver BW. The staging business application programming interfaces (BAPIs) stages the data from various database systems.

Once the data transformed, it is stored in SAP NetWeaver BW database in the physical tables. This transfer consumes more time.

However, SAP HANA has the on-the-fly cubes that pull out the data directly from the physical tables. The ETL process for the data transformation is performed on the fly as well. The analytic view creates a dynamic template or schema that is a plan establishing the stewardship on how to transform the data, rather than already having a transformed layer of data stored in the analytic view. This dynamic schema should solve the industrial problems to define dynamic schemas.

The present study was intended, in part, to research the IMDB (in-memory databases) technologies such as SAP HANA, which can handle large volumes of dataset for industrial applications. An investigation was also made of the integration with ERP systems such as SAP NetWeaver with minimum in-memory capabilities of RAM (Random access memory) on a distributed cluster technology. The classical data warehouse such as SAP NetWeaver BW has a procedural sequence of performing three steps, one after the other, known as ETL (Extract, Transform, Load). The organization will set up data governance, and data warehousing strategy based on which, for the specific scenario of BW, the ETL performed after evaluation of multiple data sources and targets. The extraction and transformation occur in SAP NetWeaver BW as the basic step, in case of a possible SAP source system, invoking the SAP BW API service leveraging API (Application Programming Interface) layer. In the case of other potential systems, where the format is non-standardized SAP format, a file interface can be leveraged. Thus, the data can be extracted in .csv format.

Tableau

Tableau a research project at Stanford University for Department of Defense turned into a commercial big data visualization product. A string of products from Tableau suit different consumers. An individual version of Tableau Desktop is offered for home computing desktops. Tableau provides several innovative capabilities for being a business intelligence platform. Corporations can leverage Tableau Server that provides accelerated pace, mobility capabilities, which is a browser-based tool that can run on the web and mobile as well. Tableau Online is the cloud-computing version of Tableau that comes with managed partner services with pre-configured solutions. Tableau Desktop version can hook to the live data in the machine. Tableau Desktop also comes with the in-memory analytics fast engine.

The fast engine is a columnar-based technology engine. Fundamentally the fast data engine technology of Tableau applies and provides interoperability on storage compression on columns speeding up the data on the main memory, thus creating chunks of columns with data instead of leveraging row-based storage. The difference is when a record in a large data set is accessed in traditional row-based storage, the scan runs throughout the table to isolate the record, thus increasing the number of input and output operations on the disk. The columnar-based storage can read the data at blazing speed. Once this data is retrieved and cached in the main memory of in-memory architecture, the data stays there for ease of access. This is very effective for accessing and processing large data sets of big data. Tableau unleashes a bevy of connectivity options to SAP BW and SAP HANA with open data connectivity driver. Tableau also provides connectivity to at least 35 other data sources to integrate databases such as Microsoft, Oracle, and IBM, etc. products. Tableau includes integration with Cloudera Hadoop, Hortonworks Hadoop distributions, MapR Hadoop Hive, and R language.

QlikView

Björn Berg and Staffan Gestrelius invented QlikView in Sweden in the early 1990s. They wanted to create visualization tool for the business intelligence that provides perspectives into the big data. One of the early adopters of QlikView was Tetrapak, a packaging corporation for food and beverages. QlikView allows the creation of visualization of data with simple drag and drop techniques with self-service capabilities without having to write many SQL queries with inner joins and outer joins to extract and discover the data. QlikView has a centralized repository of all the applications in one place. QlikView can run through a variety of database vendors to connect to a large number of data sources into QlikView. Notable data sources include SAP Sybase IQ, HP, IBM, Microsoft, Oracle, Teradata, and SAP HANA.

QlikView also has smart indexing capabilities for the search to discover new data every time for patterns and trends and supports a large number of data types. QlikView runs in-memory analytics as well. QlikView also has dashboards for creating a business context to aid decision support systems of organizations. Consumers can create groups of data aggregations by regions and segments to draw comparisons for creating analytics that lead to decision-making. The analytics can be for opportunities management and leads to customer relationship management. QlikView has integration with mobiles and tablets with HTML5 support to diffuse the disruption of mobility for customers. The geographical location service from QlikView can also track the consumers for localization of data. Similar to Tableau, QlikView has the landscape environment for quickly creating prototype solutions either for a specialty industry to handle large data sets for data sampling and collection analysis. This quick prototyping can reduce the cost of prototyping. Conventional Business Intelligence tools can take months to create a prototyping. However, QlikView can take weeks to days to create the prototyping solutions depending on the complexity of the solution to assess the feasibility of the business requirements.

Splunk

Splunk big data tool works with both structured and unstructured data. Splunk covers a range of pre-configured rapid deployment packages for ease of big data content analysis and readily pluggable for corporations to slice and dice their visualization and turn the data into valuable decision-making actionable insights for achieving operational excellence in business intelligence competency centers. Similar to Tableau and QlicView, Splunk has powerful search algorithms to search for the content and start analyzing the raw information to sophisticated outputs in the form of dashboards and report analytics.

However, Splunk takes a completely new approach for connecting to the data sources when compared to Tableau and QlikView. Splunk builds dynamic enterprise knowledge to connect from text files all the way to most complex and sophisticated data sources. Splunk schemaless or dynamic schema works perfectly for unstructured data, as it can adapt from target data schema. In essence, there is no limitation for Splunk to connect to any data source in the world of databases. Splunk delivers around more than 500 database connection applications to a bevy of databases. Leveraging open database connectivity, Java database connectivity, and several other connectivity applications, Splunk can connect to any database source without limitations. The capabilities to connect to any data sources provide the agility for Splunk to aggregate and analyze machine-generated data from various corporate data logs and index the data.

R language

R language is a freeware open to the public for tenacious statistical computing and visualization of sophisticated calculations in a graphical interface for big data and data mining. R is a programming language as well and can integrate with Apache Hadoop and

MapReduce. Recently, Microsoft acquired Revolution Analytics that manufacturers R language to integrate it with SQL Server for corporations that run Microsoft products, it would be seamless to plug and play R for large-scale projects. R language has been making strides in ever-expanding scientific fields including high-performance computing for biology and genomics with mathematical and statistical layers. Recently R announced Enterprise Editions RevoR and ScaleR commercial distributions. These packages can throttle the bottlenecks by identifying the operating capacity of the processor cores. RevoR mechanizes the throughput of the cores by self-regulating multitasking by executing a large number of threads simultaneously. ScaleR is another big data strategy that can perform truckloads of statistical predictive analytics in several industries. Media and publishing companies, Internet providers, search giants, social media, and banking industries fully tap into the potential of language R for statistical computing. By mid-2014, the number of installations jumped to two million. In a recent survey, R ranked as the top statistical computing language for big data to crunch millions of records.

Handling big data requires features that are not overly complex and after gleaning the big data result sets with MapReduce from Hadoop platform, it requires fine-tuning and performing calculations to provide the value for the big data after running a bevy of algorithms on clusters of network rack-mounted servers. Most of the high-end infrastructure creates the data result sets and the tools like R language excel in consuming the data and discover the underlying trends and patterns by turning it into valuable insights with statistical computing. In previous years, SAS and SPSS were the most popular statistical computing tools to build the *last mile* analysis. However, none of these tools created the big data revolution as much R has generated in the past decade.

IBM acquired SPSS, and Microsoft bought Revolution Analytics, and North Carolina State University founded SAS. The premises for creating these groundbreaking statistical programming languages differ with the rise of the big data analytics. The genesis of SAS was to collect, process, analyze, and synthesize the big data generated from agronomics, crops, and plants. R language is the next-generation innovation of S language. Bell Labs founded S language. C, Fortran, and R fuel the source code of R language. The roots of R show the utilization in the world of academia for research and development. In the recent times launch of RevoR and ScaleR from R has opened the gates for enterprises looking to wrangle their data. However, R has the freeware version for further development. Corporations like Google, Facebook, The New York Times, and FDA profoundly perform statistical computing with graphics on big data by R. However, R is not just a statistical computing big data tool, it is a big data programming language with advanced features such as neural networks. R rapidly embraced a larger community of big data development community in a short time blowing SAS and SPSS out of water.

R comes with several features for handling big data for various use cases:

Data collection and sampling from large data sets for R

Corporations perform statistical analysis on the total result datasets returned from Hadoop platform for discovering the insights of the big data. In certain scenarios, enterprises may have to carry out prototyping solutions to analyze the feasibility of a solution for financials, banking, media, publishing, bioinformatics, and several other industries. These industries can engage in performing the big data analysis with R without having to run the statistical analysis against the entire data set. Thus, corporations can make a choice for the usage of sample datasets for rapid prototyping solutions, as long as the magnitude of the data is in the realm of a billion data sets. However, the data procured for sampling should be unbiased that encompasses all the demographics, regions, segmentations, and channels from where the data generates. This provides the most real dimension of the data to keep the prototyping close to the requirements.

R Memory management

R requires all the objects to run on DRAM (Dynamic random access memory). A new league of high-performance computing meets R due to the need for the speed. However, on regular home computing machines that differ at the core level of operating system with 32-bit and 64-bit CPUs, the memory limitation is two gigabytes and eight terabytes of RAM. The memory constraints arise from the design of the operating system to execute arithmetic operations per cycle. Once the levee breaks, R will start dispatching premonitory messages. R language provisions various functions to determine the load size of each data set object, this way; the machine can load up the data sets that comply the threshold limits. Because the data resides on main-memory, R and SAP HANA complement each other to be able to run the large sets of data on a potential 100 TB main memory of SAP HANA.

R Parallel Computing

To run R language on a home computing machine, breaking the data into several data nuggets can optimize the devices with moderate main memory. This method works as a parallel computing procedure by parallel processing the data chunks in small groups and then combine the result sets with specific functions. However, there are specific functions that can perform such specific tasks in language R. This may not apply to large data sets that require staying in the main memory of the machine.

R's synergy with a bevy of programming languages

As of today, R language has 6700+ built-in packages covering a substantial number of operating systems and programming languages. R, ahead of its time harmonizes object-oriented programming languages such as Java and C++ as an integral part of R. There are packages within R that can enable such integration to multiple programming languages. These packages capacitate other programming languages. The source code can be written seamlessly in integrated programming languages to allow the native integration and advanced concepts with

Java and C++ to write in R. However, there could be some limitations on the usage of some of features from R when written in other languages.

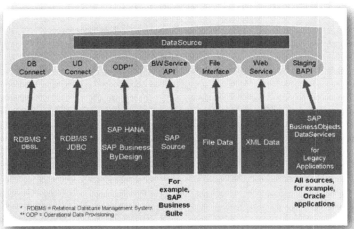

Figure 1. Data staging with several databases (SAP, 2013).

Figure 1 explains the data staging, data connect, and universal data connect to different application scenarios.

Once the data transformed, it is stored in SAP Netweaver BW database in the physical tables. The ETL process for the data transformation is performed on the fly as well. The analytic view creates a dynamic template and schema that is a plan establishing the stewardship on how to transform the data, rather than already having a transformed layer of data stored in the analytic view. This dynamic schema should solve the industrial problems to define dynamic schemas. SAP HANA overcomes these problems.

Conclusions

In the new golden age of big data with the evolution of database giants like SAP HANA, IBM, and Oracle Exadata, it is hard for a company to choose the right database. Organizations cannot easily decide about the database that provides the edge to turn their data into real world competitive advantage and actionable intelligence. While IBM DB2 Blu supports row-based and columnar storage, Oracle Exadata only supports storage with hybrid columnar compression. Though, Oracle Exadata heralds its Exadata machine, as the performance rocket with speed of thought analytics, the underlying architecture is a combination of both row-based and columnar-based storage. This is in contrast to SAP HANA columnar strategy and IBM DB2 Blu's row-columnar strategy. IBM's strategy, of dividing IBM DB2 Blu for in-memory computing and IBM's PureData for big data, has shown that IBM DB2 Blu is not enterprise-ready and big data ready integrated solution.

However, Oracle's Exadata algorithms do not compare to IBM DB2 Blu solution. IBM DB2 Blu has powerful industrial algorithms and compression ratio. Hence, Oracle might require expensive and extensive disk space as opposed to IBM DB2 Blu. Oracle is still in the process of building their next generation in-memory solution option. Oracle in-memory research was in pre-beta stage as of 2013. Therefore, Exadata is not a pure in-memory option at this time. Oracle has a separate strategy with Oracle big data appliance that shows that the database is not purely integrated as big data ready, and this is where SAP HANA achieves supremacy. Oracle also lacks the SIMD for MPP to accelerate the data with parallel processing mechanism that is provided by SAP HANA.

The present review of literature revealed an incomplete and unbalanced body of knowledge about the cost of managing computer generated data, which is very high with minimal rewards as traditional relational database management system (RDBMS) tools cannot provide what real-time data customers need in the immediate moment. An exponential big data expansion is occurring globally. As a result, organizations cannot immediately access needed data to tap into opportunities to solve complex problems relevant to informed decision-making. Lack of access to critical data based on analysis of corporate data creates missed opportunities to take necessary action either to introduce a new product, improve an existing product, or build the capabilities of the organization. Based on the lack of empirical evidence about the value of SAP HANA as an in-memory computing platform to solve the big data dilemma, the present study was an effort to to explore the big-data appliances that diffuse the speed of big data to the organizations with awareness, interest, trial, evaluation, and adoption.

Summary

Chapter 3 contains a discussion of the data collection and analysis process. Included are sections relevant to approval of the study by the California Intercontinental University Institutional Review Board, and an explanation of the origins of the secondary data that were used for the study. Included also is commentary about the instrumentation, sample selection, data collection, and data analysis efforts pertinent to the collection and analysis of the secondary data.

3

Research Method

A SYSTEMATIC STUDY WAS conducted of organizations that have pain points with their business intelligence reporting and movement of data between OLTP and OLAP. Challenges encountered by the employees of various information technology users from their perspective were studied, and solutions were proposed to solve their conundrums. The research method implemented a predefined set of _DC to delve into the platform challenges of _P and OLTP processes.

ed to this paper was based on the research half of SAP, with highly structured meth-ith predefined questionnaires with results ipants spanning the globe. The researcher esearch methodology and research analy-ry data from the IDC study. Information and business managers responsible for blending transactional applications and analytical applications to make a decision were polled in the IDC survey. The IDC sought to understand problems related to disentanglement of OLAP and OLTP due to technological limitations, performance bottlenecks from the database applications and analytics, primary information technology challenges with the latency of the transactions, and time spent for the data movement between OLTP to OLAP databases.

Research Questions

The research questions that guided this study were:

RQ1: How can SAP HANA speed up the diffusion of big data via awareness, interest, evaluation, trial, and adoption?

RQ2: Why is SAP HANA more efficient than other big data appliances such as Oracle and IBM?

RQ3: What data show that SAP HANA can shape the future of emerging growth technologies?

Case studies are included in the discussion. The research was intended to resolve performance challenges, reduce complexity of IT landscapes, more efficiently move data from OLTP to OLAP with flexibility, and reveal how speech-to-speech translation with IVR can resolve the global challenges of information delay.

Data Collection and Sampling

No permission to use human subjects for the study was required from the California Intercontinental University Institutional Review Board pursuant to the U.S. Federal Government Department of Health and Human Services (2009) regulation 45 CFR § 46.10 because the study was based on secondary data and no human subjects were involved. Regulation 45 CFR § 46.10 states the probability and magnitude of harm or discomfort anticipated in the research should not be greater in and of themselves than any ordinarily encountered in daily life, or during the performance of routine physical or psychological examinations or tests.

It was assumed that the methodology of the IDC study was accurate and the results substantiated by the data collection and analysis. The IDC held interviews with various IT departments to separate the reality of SAP HANA from the hype market that has been generated with results from SAP customers. The results were published by SAP at the convention of SAP Slovenia and Croatia Innovations event in September 2012. The present study was based on those results.

IDC was the researcher. IDC is also prominent among all organizations in data intelligence trends and researches new technologies in the marketplace. IDC engages 1,100 analysts in over 110 countries helping clients set up strategic and operational competencies to run their businesses with long term strategic planning. IDC gathered case studies from SAP by using the data to illustrate the advantages of having a single database platform for the enterprises. IDC gathered the data from a survey sponsored by SAP, with 759 participants of worldwide geographical composition. The survey had approximately 405 information technology managers, and 352 other managers responsible for business services in organizations. The business and IT managers responded by citing the challenges they were encountering in their organizations dealing with multiple database platforms. IDC probed into the data gathered from the survey for analysis. It examined how SAP HANA can act as a single database platform for real-time OLTP that constitute systems of transactions, and OLAP that are systems of analytic processing for reporting purposes for decision-support systems. IDC had conducted a web survey over 1002 global participants, translated into four different languages. The participants were C(Chief)-level exeuctives for business units, and business and IT managers.

Data Analysis

IDC conducted interviews with the aid of a survey questionnaire. The questionnaire could also be used to build reusable business use cases for various industries with the introduction of effective big data technologies. The sample use cases reported by the IDC were in the form of responses to surveys and questionnaires, which contained closed-ended questions, applied with a pre-defined set of procedures. The extracted data from IDC survey results was very comprehensive covering various types of departments and employees. The data was gathered from manufacturing, supply chain, logistics, finance, marketing, R&D, and customer service departments. These business functions represent the core of realistic SAP ERP, SAP SCM, and SAP CRM implementations.

The data gathered from the survey showed information delays from the ad hoc reports for each department in the organizations. The data gathered from such a large sample of industries can be reapplied to any other organization with similar business operations with or without global presence. The survey had a stable design from the beginning to the end and identified the business operations that have become ungovernable, disorderly, and chaotic due to the technological limitations to process variety of data types and massive volumes of big data.

Summary

Chapter 3 outlined the design and basic procedures underlying this study. The design selected served to determine the answers to the research questions. Furthermore, this chapter included a discussion on the appropriateness of the design in addressing the above relationships; research questions stated in Chapter 1, instrumentation, sample selection, data collection, and data analysis efforts motivating the conclusions of this study.

4

Findings and Results

SAP HANA REINVIGORATED many organizations by resolving performance challenges, reducing of complexity of IT landscapes, improved flexibility in moving data from OLTP systems to OLAP systems, and meeting the challenges of information delays. Forty percent of survey respondents to the IDC survey were in business organizations that required more than 48 hours to close their financials for analytical purposes. At least 25% of the business users thought the information delays had significantly affected their business and created inflexibility to proactively counter the dynamic needs of the business models in the organization. The time spent on moving the data from traditional RDBMS to an OLAP system was reported as enormous. Seventy percent of their time was spent in extracting, transforming, and loading the data from the RDBMS OLTP system to the OLAP system.

Empirical Data from IDC

Business transactions need not be silos running on different data platforms and different enterprise software technologies. The reporting and analytics analysis to perform on such multiple platforms can introduce a high margin of error. The lack of data integrity between platforms requires weeks or months of manual operations to combine the data to produce the accurate outputs in disentangled transactional and analytical platforms.

There are several benefits customers can derive from an integrated platform. In an organization that is running with hundreds of software business applications and databases, there is a high rate of platform change. This increases the complexity of upgrades to the enterprise applications and integrating the data in multiple cycles. Information delays in the data transfers can introduce delayed decision-making, creating a loss of edge needed to counter competitors in the marketplace. Several change requests in the enterprise can result in resistance by the employees to go through a huge curve of change management that disrupts productivity in the business. Business leaders need instant insights into the data, business processes, and the latest status of service tickets, transactions, and interaction logs with customers. SAP CRM powered by HANA has boosted the acceleration of searches performed on the inboxes.

Employees of organizations have several decisions to make to ensure customer loyalty and boost revenues by providing discounts and resolving issues with services and products. SAP HANA boosts performance allowing the employees to search the inbox easily to extract needed data. It triggers any workflow notifications to other employees who are in the process chain to perform the actions and run interactive analytics reports so they can analyze the data that can lead to informed decision-making.

Real-time visibility into customer's demands can provide near-accurate analytical reports that can lead to improvements in the revenues generated. SAP CRM powered by HANA can improve the business processes of the organization to sell products and services more efficiently. The SAP 360 customer is a product accelerated by HANA on the SAP CRM platform to enable a 360-degree view of the sales activity. SAP HANA on SAP CRM platform has shown 115 times more improvements in performance and response time of the UI to increase the organizational capabilities. The improved, accelerated inbox search capabilities have shown 100% improvement in terms of finding the faxes, letters, and other artifacts from the inbox with SAP HANA attribute and calculation views. SAP CRM loyalty management has shown significant performance improvements by 10 times. The SAP CRM Interaction center with CTI and IVR has shown five times improvement. From a strategic perspective, the entanglement of OLAP and OLTP as a single database can drastically reduce the total cost of ownership (TCO) by having a single worldwide database.

Businesses require transformation to improve the way they conduct transactions by optimizing and simplifying business processes. SAP HANA can accelerate the organizational transformation by building best business practices. Data driven business processes such as revenue management, pipeline management, opportunity management, activities, and task management in SAP CRM can be improved dramatically. SAP SCM requires advanced planning and optimization. SAP HANA can provide predictive analytics for complex calculations. Faster time-to-value on the ROI and reduced exposure to risk can allow the organization to lead the competition.

In a February 2013 HANA article published by IDC sponsored by SAP, IDC reported the conduct of several surveys with Information Technology leaders in various. Ideally, the financial closing activities are expected to happen in a few hours at the month's end. Reporting the financial data is crucial for understanding an enterprise's financial position in the market. However, 40% of the participants in the IDC survey revealed that it is taking approximately 48 hours or more to prepare a report based on financial data. In the business units of the respondents, 25% revealed they were looking for some accelerated information explosion for decision-making in the business.

The systems in an enterprise operate in silos. The supply chain operations occur in multiple systems, consolidating the planning activities into a single system, a herculean task. The pricing, costing analysis requirements are run globally from different regions, thus generating structured and unstructured formats from XML files, flat files, and tab delimited files. The inventory adjustments occur in one system, and the pricing is set up in another system; this creates information delays for physical inventory adjustments.

The disentanglement of the platforms can create multiple databases and multiple patterns of the structures. For this reason the transactional platforms and analytical platforms cannot be different. The lack of historical trend analysis makes the demand planning more complex delimiting gaining insights into the analytics of the information. The database sometimes is stored in excel spreadsheets; loss of spreadsheets can also further delay the information for decision-making. There is also a synchronization problem between multiple platforms; the data either does not tie up with other system or is out of synch with other systems. The acceleration of business processes is directly related to the accelerated performance of the database, the integration of multiple database platforms, and creating a unique structured format for ease of analytical purposes. The separated transactional and analytical platforms create information delays, and the time consumed in extraction, loading, and transformation into a new format creates severe latency.

IDC conducted the survey with more than 400+ IT managers involving several departments of the organizations polled such as finance and controlling, logistics, sales and distribution, customer relationship management, quality management systems, and supply chain management systems. The survey revealed that the migration of the data took more than 24 hours in approximately 50% of the cases. The other 50% revealed that it took 48 hours for data migration from one platform to another. A large number of cases also revealed that the waiting period was ranging between seven and 10 days. The new data gets created from the transactional platform, and by the time the analytical platform compiles the data, the data is already out of synch at the time of finalization of analysis.

One research question in the IDC study was to determine, on average, how much time it took for the movement of the data from transactional platform to analytical platform, unlike SAP HANA platform that has both transactional and analytical instances on a single platform. The average time spent varied from less than an hour to more than an 11 days to extract and migrate the data from structured and unstructured formats and prepare in a standardized format for analytical purposes for processes in the organization. Respondents' population was represented on a percentage basis. The IDC survey was conducted with a population of 407 respondents.

The fragmentation of the database systems can cause significant delays in terms of financial closing and month end activities. The power users of the business struggle in spending weeks to compile the data and running processes from transactional platforms to analytical platforms. However, to the dismay of the IDC, the survey, with a population sample of 352, revealed that the business users were content with such disintegrated systems. The IDC survey has defined scale to indicate the satisfaction. The scale was rated from one to five. Scale one indicated no satisfaction and scale five indicated the highest level of satisfaction. The IDC survey represents the scale of satisfaction on Y-axis and percentage of a number of respondents on the X axis. Of a total of 40% respondents, 35% rated the satisfaction with a rating of four.

In another research survey conducted by IDC in the IT departments in the same enterprise for a population of 407 IT business users, for operationalization of report requests,the survey measurd the time spent on preparing for extraction of the data from the transactional platform, and moving the data to analytical platform for fulfilling requests. The time was indicated on the X axis in terms of hours and days, and the Y axis represents the percentage of the respondents. On a scale of total 40%, 30% of the respondents mentioned it takes one to two days to complete the operational report or a specific request.

Prior research revealed that the limitations of technology to move the data from unstructured systems to analytical database is one problem, and the refresh cycles of new data flooding into transactional databases can keep the analytical database completely out of synch. The traditional OLAP RDBMS systems that do not have the columnar storage to respond quickly and are not designed to process the avalanche of the data in a timely manner, and for this reason, completely lose the real-time visibility of the data. Organizations cannot make a higher-level management decision based on a report generated by logistics or supply chain from the data that was populated few days ago. The dynamic shift of the business goods movement, shipping, transportation, and sales cannot be captured in real-time in disintegrated platforms. Each OLTP system has its own database schema, and some of the systems are even stored on an access database. Some of the OLTP systems in an organization are not even part of RDBMS design. These unstructured data systems will require a big data application to standardize the data. The large volumes of data is another conundrum for the business, as the OLAP and OLTP systems that are not tightly integrated can lose the granularity of the data for predictive analytics and performing simulations of advanced planning optimization for demand forecasting, and supply network collaboration.

The IDC survey showed the complexities experienced by the business users due to the disintegrated platforms. The IDC considered the technological limitations in the organization, such as (a) lack of predictive analysis and simulations; (b) challenges of working with big data and gargantuan volumes of data; (c) gaining granularity on data for profitability analysis and financial statements; (d) self-service capabilities for reports and analytics creation for the business organization, and; (e) performing intelligent searches capable of streamlining queries with specific extracts. The IDC survey results in the population of 407 business user respondents in depicting the tasks they cannot complete on Y axis, triggered by the technological limitations and percentage of respondents represented on X axis. Over 40% of the respondents in the SAP survey indicated that the systems do not have the capability of predictive analytics, simulations, and visibility to real-time access to the data.

Ten years ago it was not possible to have an integrated, unified database management system that supports both OLAP and OLTP. Many research studies concluded that it was not a feasible option for organizations with complex business processes. The database information systems are state-of-the-art technology for decision support systems. Organizations conduct business on a daily basis for operationalization of their processes; this bulk volume of data is created on OLTP systems. OLAP systems are used for database mining techniques and generate analytical reports for informed decision-making in the enterprise.

A decade ago, the underlying database structures for analytical processing were created entirely on a different architectural basis, as opposed to online transaction processing. At times, when foreign exchange transactions are extracted, transformed, and loaded back into online analytical processing systems for analytical purposes, the currency rates fluctuated and the real-time visibility of the data was lost. The process involved to extract, transform, and load from OLTP to OLAP was not only time intensive, the process also had some significant latency when transferred from OLTP to OLAP.

The OLTP systems store the atomic values in single independent fields of transactional system, whereas OLAP systems have different structures that can support the aggregation, and summarization of the transactions to represent key figures for reporting and analytics. The systems also represent different business objectives. The OLTP systems represent operationalization of business transactions. The OLAP systems were created to support the decision-making of the organization. The biggest research question a decade ago was "Is it possible to have a unified database management platform that blends both OLTP and OLAP systems without latency, and near real-time accuracy?"

Jones[13] reasoned that OLTP and OLAP database platforms should be separated. OLTP atomic structures have a normalized design complying with RDBMS principles. However, OLAP systems do not have such normalized database designs as it contains a summary and aggregation of calculations. The structures do not tend to perfectly align the way OLTP structures were created. Bontempo and Zagelow[14] posited that there are differences between OLTP and OLAP systems in terms of hosting elastic and inelastic data, and impromptu data extraction versus predictive analytics on OLAP systems. Thomas and Datta[15] argued the logical and physical, architectural designs are completely different between OLTP and OLAP; therefore, they are not consistent and require different database design models and architecture. The OLTP environment mostly designed as a highly normalized landscape to store atomicity of the data values in each field to reduce the redundancy of the database.

Barbusinki stated that a unified database management platform is not possible. Howson[16] concluded that relational online analytical processing (ROLAP) and multidimensional online analytical processing (MOLAP) differ from each other due to the difference in physical structures. The combination may reduce the ability to query them seamlessly. Through the evolution of SQL3, ROLAP was a reality in terms of supporting multi-dimensional objects in a normalized database system. Various database management vendors, when implementing SQL3, expanded the functionality such that MOLAP applications were working similar to ROLAP. Researchers have reached a conclusion that a single database management model or platform cannot support the needs of OLTP and OLAP.

Five years later Hasso[17] mentioned the possibility of building a blended database management system that could work for both OLTP and OLAP. Fundamentally, there are architectural differences between OLTP and OLAP though both are based on an RDBMS design. The difference comes from the technicalities of tuples that are arranged in the pattern of rows and stored in a number of blocks. As the database query is fired to fetch the data, the data is retrieved from these blocks (that are stored on disks) by performing disk operations and bringing it to the buffers of cache memory. The indexing is one of the mechanisms involved to speed up the retrieval with a specific key or combination of keys to faster retrieval of data. However, the data on OLAP systems is stored in star schemas. The columns can be compressed to accelerate the retrieval of the database. A recent development to store the data in a columnar pattern has boosted the retrieval of data to pull the required columns based on the parameters targeting specific columns.

Organizations require a seamless database system that can combine both OLTP and OLAP on a single database management system to match the planned, and actual values for financials, supply chain planning, and logistics to get near real-time results. Moore's (1968) law has proved time and again the process clock has been doubling every 18 months, keeping in view the latest multi-core and multi-threaded CPU servers architecture for caching of 'main-memory,' columnar storage has a high advantage for accelerated data retrieval.

A German brewery company conducted a prototype speed test. The data sample included five years worth of SAP data. The data source was pointing to the SAP financial table. The table contained 160 columns with one million tuples. The total table size was estimated to be at 35 GB. When this data was extrapolated to columnar data storage, the size was compressed to 8 GB due to the compression algorithms performed on columnar database storage. It was proved that columnar storage has showed 100 – 1000 factor of performance gains as opposed to the row based storage.

Row-based storage contains non-compressed data; the calculations executed on such data take a while to run analytical reports. The raw data requires a higher number of algorithms to operate in extracting the data and pulling it in chunks into the 'main-memory.' To leverage the distributed infrastructure of multi cores on the CPU, the compressed data requires splitting into a number of chunks to spread it across the cores with a parallel processing mechanism. The parallel processing of the columns divided into chunks can significantly boost the scan operations executed on the attributes. In case of row-based storage, the calculations of foreign transactions with currency conversions, quantities to deal with the inventory adjustments, and date ranges for billing revenue items, requires row-by-row calculation, which would take a significant amount of time. However, the column-based storage does not overload the central core as the load on each core is minimal and independent as it is executed at the tuple level with parallel processing mechanism synchronously for each tuple. This reduces the amount of synchronization between multiple cores. The rapid spawning of parallelism on multiple cores eliminates the need for any indexing operations that need to be performed on each row.

In SAP OLAP systems such as SAP BW, SAP BI, the prototype was conducted on four of SAP customers to review the change documents and logs generated with delta updates. Plattner classified the results into *aggregate*, *status*, and *value updates*. Aggregate updates are common and heavy in automotive, financial, media, and utility industries. In SAP ERP system, financial accounting and controlling modules go through some heavy updates. The study showed the row-based database applications experienced degradation in performance. However, the number of instances for aggregation appeared to be running at ultra-blazing speed on column-based OLAP systems.

The SAP ERP system captures the status changes to any transactions such as billing, invoicing, and deliveries to indicate the status changes at each stage. Since these changes are massive in the system, the column-based OLAP system can keep these changes in uncompressed format to boost the speed of the system. Value updates in the SAP ERP system can occur on the actual changes of each field in any business transaction. SAP tracks these changes with old and new values as materialized views of changes.

To have a blended OLAP and OLTP system, the inserts need to occur at blazing speed and the tuples must be stored with a high compression ratio to push and pull into the main-memory cache rapidly, providing significant benefits to the business. Business management teams from the IDC survey answered questions with respect to weighing the benefits for each of their departments. The survey was conducted on 352 participants. Most of the pain points raised by the business participants dealt with accelerated speed, the accuracy of the data, and granularity of the data for analysis purposes. The accuracy is currently disrupted because the data are distributed on multiple database systems. The accuracy is impacted as the data goes through various formats before it gets analyzed on the analytical platform, thus losing data integrity. The structures of the databases do not support a deeper granularity in today's world as the design does not support building on the fly cubes for dynamic transformations.

SAP HANA launched by SAP AG has been proved to be the solution for having a blended OLAP and OLTP database management system. A unified database management system has advantages. It can blend the transactional system that is used as a system of record for back office functionality as well as an executive decision system for supporting the decision-making processes, both based on the fact-driven logic from the analytical reports. The unified database management system can support real-time decision-making based on the state of affairs in the company without having to wait a number of days to transform the data. The near real-time accuracy is only possible when the large chunks of data can be compressed and cached into the main-memory as and when the data requires analysis.

Based on IDC study, approximately 60% of the respondents from business, as opposed to IT, answered that the information delays between OLTP systems to OLAP environment were not unsatisfactory and they could live with such information delays. One of the fundamental reasons for such satisfaction around information delays is that the respondents could not think of a possible answer, and they have prepared their downstream systems and the business managers to live with such information delays and set the expectations that the analytical reports cannot be ready within an expected time frame.

In another survey, the IDC tried to understand the rationale behind such information delays, and how critical this data is for decision making within enterprises. They asked if businesses get the information in real-time, what benefits the organization could have in terms of supply chain cycles, manufacturing activities, and on-time support for dynamic business models. Results showed critical objectives of the business can be met when near real-time data and near accuracy of information can support rapidly evolving dynamic business models. The survey was conducted on 352 business managers. Reviewing the possibility of having a blended system, the data can be available when the business needs to take a decision, rather than waiting for the data to be available, which would decrease opportunities lost in the marketplace versus opportunities won. Sometimes, rightful data is all that is needed for making a decision for a business model at right time. Of 352 respondents, 50% mentioned that the right data at the right time would provide them with the ability to transform the business processes more rapidly outdistance the competition. Results clearly showed that the business managers in organizations cognizant of the fact that speed of the data can transform the business process rapidly and increase revenues for the organization.

IT departments face several challenges because OLTP and OLAP systems are disentangled resulting in slow performance issues. The world needs a database that can optimize the database operations workload on an integrated database platform. There are four components that are of importance in such a process as is described in the following paragraphs.

The OLTP database, in the traditional sense, serves as a system of OLTP to store the volume of business transactions occurring in the system on a daily with a high volume per second. The physical database requires various types of data attributes to be stored, normalization of the table relationships, elimination of redundant de-normalized database attributes, indexing in a traditional RDBMS, clustering, and pooling of database tables. SAP ERP, CRM, SRM, SCM, and PLM systems support the OLTP database, as an example.

OLAP database systems are built to support the decision-making of the organization and preserve historical information for running predictive analytics and data mining. Over the decades, enterprises rely on two types of data in the organization, i.e., fixed data, dynamic data. Some of the master data stays static throughout the lifecycle of an organization. SAP BI is an example of OLAP database. In a disentangled OLTP and OLAP databases, the data is heavily duplicated from OLTP to OLAP to transform the data for analytical purposes. OLAP database structures are created differently from traditional OLTP system with multi-dimensional arrays and star schemas.

In disentangled database systems, an ETL process was required to move the database from OLTP to OLAP or SAP BI system. In recent times, SAP, IBM, and Oracle have enabled the unified database management systems to have OLTP and OLAP in one system. Some have multiple OLTP systems for finance, human resources, enterprise resource planning, and supply chain management system. These multiple sources result from a complex extraction, transformation, and loading process into OLAP database. As the blended database system is on the rise, the need for ETL process is continuing to diminish. Now, OLAP database design sits on top of the OLTP database design.

An OLTP transaction must be ACID compliant. The transaction must be atomic in terms of rolling back to the original stage of the database in case of a network disaster, power blackouts, or outages. The transaction saved should result in a complete status of the transaction without any pending status. Pending database updates have a consistency in the system of record. Regardless, a parallel mechanism can allow transactions to occur concurrently. The state of one transaction should be processed independently of another transaction. The transactions that are complete and saved to the database should not result in loss of data, regardless of any new transactions that are added to the database to keep the durability of the transaction.

SAP BI architecture requires running queries against the OLAP database, which is isolated from OLTP database. A unified database management system such as SAP HANA can accelerate the BI query. From the ROI perspective, two databases require an extensive number of resources to maintain the database at OLTP and OLAP levels, in addition to the number of middleware systems required for transforming the data through ETL process. The database size significantly increases, maintaining similar patterns of the data in different structures in two separate database management systems. This also results in maintaining multiple landscapes and SAP instances, multiple security models, and multiple designs to secure the data from various sources and ETL middleware.

SAP HANA resolves the challenges faced by IT departments by providing a blended transactional and analytical system. It provides the optimization of OLAP database queries and a process to transform the data. All the ACID compliant INSERT, UPDATE, and DELETE database operations occurring on OLTP do not slow down the system's performance in the blended database management system. Data reads are significantly improved on SAP HANA because the data is cached in the main-memory, which reduces the input and output operations significantly on the database.

In 2013, some SAP HANA performance benchmarks were released that still require SAP America's audit. SAP HANA scans the database at 3 MB per microsecond per each core on a multi-core 80-core server, which is 240 GB per second for each node. The insert operations on HANA database are at 1.5 million records per second on each core or 120 million records per second on each node. The aggregation happens at 12 million records per second on each core or 960 million records on each node. This shows a clear improvement of 100 times over disk-based scan systems.

With a blended OLTP and OLAP database, once the transactions that are saved to the HANA database, data automatically moves and populates into BI data structures as part of the delta merge process. For static data, BI report query can scan the database relevant to OLTP, when trying to access near real-time database. The scan operations will scan both OLTP and OLAP portions. This has some significant acceleration in terms of accessing the memory from the cache as opposed to accessing it from the disk-based systems. The blended database system SAP HANA not only has resolved the problem of keeping OLTP and OLAP database on the same database instance, but the automatic transfer of data from OLTP to BI, for reporting purposes, is seamless. The ability to query directly from OLTP database also gives near real-time results. SAP HANA also provides self-service BI reporting capabilities that allow the business to execute the BI reports directly without the need of the IT department personnel.

The above IDC survey results show that the isolated OLTP and OLAP systems are a big disadvantage to business organizations.

The disconnected systems create an inflexible database system and cause potential problems with redundant data duplication. The top rated challenges by the IT organizations show rigid systems, disk-based systems, gargantuan volumes, and the migration of data from OLTP system to OLAP system on a regular basis. The complexity tops the chart with 21% of respondents rating it as a challenge for the IT organization.

The fundamental problems in an organization stem from the complex data environments with multiple data sources and multiple data types. The organization needs a system that is elastic to respond to the dynamic business models and needs a single global process to support the global rollouts and regions. This can only be achieved when the database design is simplified with blended database management system such as SAP HANA.

Running the SAP BW platform requires re-platforming to SAP HANA to reduce the complexity of redundant database designs. The roadmap for deployment should begin with SAP BW 7.3 SPS07 and SAP HANA support pack stack (SPS03), or SAP BW 7.4 to SAP HANA SPS07. The business downtime from SAP BW traditional RDBMS to the SAP HANA database is minimal. Once the data migration completes from SAP BW to SAP HANA, the organization will have underlying database platform as SAP HANA. The system can be copied in SAP NetWeaver 7.3 in a single run with ABAP or ABAP+Java dual stack systems. In homogenous system copy procedure, the original database, and operating system are retained from the source to the target. In the case of migration to SAP HANA database, heterogeneous system copy is performed to copy the source database and operating system to different target database or operating system as intended. The system copy is performed to clone a source system to a target system. The database copy is performed to copy the source database to the target database system.

SAP to simplify the data migration process with heterogeneous system copy has provided rapid deployment solutions (RDS) for some specific industries that can help migrate the data with a defined preset of configured services data sets to simplify the process. This rapid deployment solution enables the flexibility with data modeling for reduction of redundant database design and brings accelerated speed in running the reporting.

One of the first steps to migrate the database from SAP BW RDBMS to SAP HANA is to prepare the infrastructure of the target system by setting up a primary application server (PAS) and the HANA database appliance server. The target server PAS will consist of BW related applications, and the HANA server hosts the in-memory database for HANA. SAP has certified hardware partners with pre-installed HANA software on the server. The business requirements, the volumes of the transactions, and scope of the reporting will define the sizing required for SAP HANA system. This report provides the resource requirements to run the HANA database, compression ratio, and table type specific compression factors. It also provides sizing effects of concept of non-active data, memory sizing, disk sizing, and CPU sizing.

The report /SDF/HANA_BW_SIZING runs on the logical maps of the ABAP data dictionary attributes and computes the physical database size stored in the database. The report performs sampling of the database by taking a few random samples of the database records and then determines the total volume stored in a database table. It also evaluates the size of the database table. The report shows the database cached into ABAP runtime memory with which to size the compression ratio required for each database table. The report indicates the tables that are required for staying in row-based storage as well as the tables that require conversion to columnar-based format.

The number of tables for a transactional commit is determined by the report to see which can be handled with a parallel process mechanism. The number of workload processes for parallel process mechanism is evaluated by this report. The report shows the degree of parallelism that needs to be enabled to allocate the dialog processes, and works process IDs into each thread. The dialog processes have limitations in terms of the run time they have. Once the dialog processes have crossed the threshold of the time limit, they are timed out. However, the basis profile parameter rdisp/max wprun_ time needs to be reset to zero to avoid time-out issues and abnormal process terminations (abends).

Complex and costly IT landscape has been a top concern for most of IT personnel. This is because there are several infrastructure landscapes with different hardware vendors due to the creation of a variety of database footprints in each organization with different OLTP and OLAP systems. Having SAP HANA as a strategic database, and an infrastructure platform with a SAP certified hardware vendor can minimize the complexity of several landscapes in the organization. A clear strategy for the creation of a data center and networking with SAP router can have long-term benefits. In most cases, when the organization purchases HANA appliance from a SAP certified hardware vendor, it comes with a blended hardware and pre-configured software solution. The support provided by SAP on the certified hardware platform ensures a run with multiple instances of HANA databases on sandbox, development, quality, and other testing servers, which serve as non-production environments on a single-node SAP HANA appliance. However, SAP does not support running multiple instances of SAP HANA on production environments.

The certified hardware provides pre-installed, pre-configured SAP HANA. There are still some on-premise activities that need to be performed to complete the post-installation steps such as installing the solution manager diagnostics (SMD) agent, connecting the SAP HANA system to the systems landscape directory (SLD). The existing standard InfoCubes need to be converted to the SAP HANA columnar-based store with a logical index created on top of it. These InfoCubes then turn into SAP HANA optimized InfoCubes. The SAP HANA database is now constructed on ABAP stack. When SAP NetWeaver BW system is migrated to SAP HANA system, dual-stack migration in a single instance is not supported. The migration needs to occur in multiple stacks by separating ABAP stack and Java stack with SLT tools. SAP supports migration of several RDBMS databases to target SAP HANA database such as DB2, MS SQL, and Oracle.

Complexities also arise from the economies of the flash perspective. DRAM memory used by SAP HANA is an upscale alternative, as opposed to classical RDBMS disk-based systems. Several alternative emerging growth memory solutions explored as part of future memory technologies can replace DRAM. The main features of future memory solutions consist of power consumption, cost, time to market, density, scaling, and performance. NAND (Not AND), 3D NAND (three dimensional not and), PCRAM (phase-change memory), STT-RAM (spin-transfer torque random access memory), and ReRAM (resistive random-access memory) are the future memory alternatives to DRAM (dynamic random access memory). The alternatives of using DDP (dual die package), TSV (through-silicon via) in DRAM have cost ramifications. TSV has a projected cost value of 22% higher than DDP.

One of the other challenges mentioned by the IT personnel in the IDC study was the large volume of data stored in a traditional RDBMS system. This can result in slow performance issues in the system. One of the preliminary activities to conduct for the migration of the data is to identify the redundant data and eliminate the data migration to SAP HANA appliance. BW data can be cleansed by reorganizing the BEx (Business explorer) bookmarks, and broadcaster bookmarks. Aggregate tables are the only feature of SAP NetWeaver BW RDBMS system, and no longer supported by SAP HANA system. The export does not occur for these database tables. Hence, deletion of these database tables prior to database export does not result in any adverse results and will minimize the footprint of the database size of the export. The database in BW also can have several unwanted application logs. These can be deleted as well. There are several systems connected to SAP BW. These can flow the data through IDocs (intermediate document). These can be archived for any auditing needs of the organization, and the links between the ALE (Application link enabling) and the IDocs can be de-chained.

As of this dissertation, retail businesses depend on availability of data to make decisions for increasing the supply chain planning operations. The velocity of the data can be an avalanche to be handled by disk-based systems. This will reduce the inventory adjustments in the organization. It improves the logistics orders and predicts the availability-to-promise (ATP) in the market more accurately by resolving the slow performance issues of the system with the SAP HANA appliance. The complexity of multiple databases, landscapes not only can add to the complexity of data flows between multiplesystems, but also can increase the cost tremendously. To work on such heterogeneous systems requires multiple upgrades on a periodical basis, and remapping of the interfaces due to the new fields from the upgrades. The organization requires a strategic approach to single global process, and single global database instance to reduce the footprint of the complexity of the landscapes.

SAP NetWeaver BW on HANA can enable tighter integration controls and simplify the process hurdles for performing data conversions and data migrations with SAP BODS. With SAP BOBJ (business objects) metadata management, several black box and white box prototypes that can be performed on BW workspaces. SAP NetWeaver BW powered by HANA can boost the speed on Webi, BEx, and Xcelsius reporting tools. It can provide the flexibility and empower the business users to run self-service BI capable reports without having to involve IT teams to build and execute the reports. Re-platforming SAP BW on HANA does not require extensive organizational change management. The entire SAP BW operations remain the same for the business users from SAP HANA, the only difference being the reports now run faster. The minimal impact to change management and organizational training makes it a safe bet for many organizations to jump to SAP HANA and quickly accelerate the systems.

The other IT challenge experienced by the business users in the IDC survey was the security of the data proliferation. SAP HANA retains and supports the BW analysis authorization roles and security models, on top of the retention of authorization concepts. SAP HANA also seamlessly integrates with SAP NetWeaver IDM (identity management) for building some robust corporate-wide security strategies.

Empirical Data from SAP on SAP HANA Customers

SAP released their SAP HANA research results of surveys, personal interviews with various industries IT business analysts, architects, managers, and other heads at the SAP Slovenia and Croatia Innovations event in September 2012. Client organization Asian Paints has achieved data volume compression ratio of 6:1 from a traditional RDBMS database to SAP HANA. The average query performance has shown a 15 times improvement over traditional RDBMS queries with a maximum query improvement up to 266 times. With the SAP Data services bolted on SAP HANA, the data load time has been reduced by an average of 95%.

Yazaki, a global automotive parts supplier, was able to power and boost their finance and controlling processes with SAP HANA. Southern Edison, an electricity and utility company, was able to load their data for conversions and data loads 5 times faster than previous RDBMS solutions. The time taken to produce the reporting results has improved 14 times on average with the overall improvement of the system as a result. SAP CRM accelerated with SAP HANA produced 75% of time-savings in response times. Overall database compression has been improved by 7.5 times. Lenovo, a computer manufacturing company, improved their shipping times with the expedited reporting. The reporting response times were improved by 20 times. SAP HANA database has shown a compression of two times from SAP BW RDBMS database. SAP BW query execution performance times were improved by 60 times.

T-Mobile, before implementing SAP HANA, was suffering from bigger business conundrums without insight into customer acquisition costs or subscription costs. The earlier T-Mobile big data solution was unable to provide insights and provided wrong analysis results. T-Mobile is a telecommunications organization with typical data sources in multiple locations, multiple formats from retail stores; call centers, including data from text messages. SAP HANA powered a marketing campaign solution of T-Mobile. That helped T-Mobile implement new retention strategies with the results of $10 to $25 savings to win-back the subscription customer base, resulting in some billions of additional revenues per year. The high-octane SAP HANA database engine has improved the analysis times by 56 times for T-Mobile. Previously, with traditional RDBMS, T-Mobile was spending a week to analyze two billion records for over two million customers. Implementation of SAP HANA and building an agile data mart has resulted in a reduction of analysis times to three hours from a week.

Provimi, a consumer products based company, was suffering from lack of informed decision-making and demand forecasting. The sales were dependent on the analytics of IT boosted by the reporting analytics. The lack of availability of insights into monthly financial closing activities resulted in time delays for making the decision on sales and projections for demand forecasting. SAP HANA was able to get Provimi up and running in a span of three weeks by accelerating their controlling and profitability analysis (CO-PA) and Enterprise Resourcing Planning (ERP) module of SAP ERP solution. The results instantly increased their profitability by providing informed decisions to plan the advanced planning optimization and demand forecasting for procuring raw materials. The results showed a capital reduction of 500,000 euros within the first week and a significant boost of 40% monthly closing activities. The analytics were boosted by 15,000 times.

Mitsui Knowledge Industry (MKI), a cancer research institute, was able to identify the cancer Deoxyribonucleic Acid (DNA) variants in 20 minutes as opposed to the earlier identification time of 3 days, resulting 216 times faster results. Charite, a Berlin-based hospital, was able to improve their diagnostic results by pattern detection. SAP HANA implementation on Charite information systems resulted in analyzing 300 million records in the span of five seconds. Cisco, a network infrastructure and router devices company, was able to make predictions about customer purchasing patterns in different seasons and was able to complete the seasonal analysis in about two to 10 seconds when run by SAP HANA. American Aerospace, a defense technology company owned by Lockheed Martin, was able to augment labor fulfillment.

ROI Benefits

The total student debt in the US is estimated by American student associations to be between $902 billion and $1 trillion. Per statistics from 2013, it was shown that each American student has graduated with a significant debt of $29,000. Some of the universities charge this premium to run their data warehouse systems that process student loans, and project interest rates. The University of Kentucky has 28,000 students on average. It has vowed to improve the graduation rate and reduce the constant increase in the tuition fees. The University of Kentucky has moved away from their traditional RDBMS database to the SAP HANA in-memory database. IDC conducted a research study. The findings of the ROI shows $6.17 million savings over a period of 5 years and a total of 509% ROI on SAP HANA implementation. The payback of the licensing, acquisition, and implementation costs happened within 9 months. The University of Kentucky has shown savings of $210,000 per year in terms of the hiked tuition fees over a period of 5 years. The challenges resolved for the University of Kentucky are nothing short of amazing.

The University of Kentucky personnel experienced 420 times improvement in speed of data warehousing reporting, as opposed to their traditional RDBMS data warehousing system. The queries were faster on HANA database and showed an improvement of 15 times in loading the data. Compressing the data with a ratio of 77% over legacy RDBMS row-based store data has eliminated the redundancy of data. The time spent in movement of data between OLTP to OLAP system was reduced by 87% and improved the

ETL processes. SAP HANA has showed running queries in real-time with an improved rate of 80% instant updates and results on analytical reports.

This has empowered the personnel of the University of Kentucky to have deeper granularity of the reporting. It has reduced the time spent in generating analytical reports, and the granularity of the data has revcealed those students who require special services and need to go through a rigorous process of preparations on specific subjects, topics,and semesters. It has improved the retention of the students because it is a preventative approach. The reduction in the attrition was directly relational to generating more revenues as the percentage of the graduation rate significantly boosted for getting their graduation clearance forms.

Innovative Improvement of BW Performance

SAP NetWeaver BW powered by HANA has improved perfor-mance for several industries such as beverages, utilities, and auto-motive. Red Bull was one of the pioneering beverage organizations that installed a SAP HANA in-memory database as early as 2011 on their existing IT landscape of SAP NetWeaver BW. The data migration from SAP BW to SAP HANA ensured business continu-ity and ensured completion of a rapid closure within 2 weeks of the project start date. The database was worth 1.5 TB before exporting from RDBMS database to HANA database. The compression rate of the data reduction resulted in 80% improvement after importing RDBMS database into SAP HANA database resulting into 0.3 TB on SAP HANA database. The architecture has ensured a zero foot-print of InfoCubes that act as an aggregation intermediary layer on SAP HANA database. Direct reads from DSO were made possible.

The replication of data flowing to InfoCubes has been eliminated, and building BWA index has been removed.

CIR food is an Italian food-catering corporation running approximately 1,100 centers in Italy and the US. In the recent years, CIR food has seen a massive surge in the demand for the food from various restaurants and educational institutions. It had challenges in performing predictive analysis for supply chain management in getting the most optimized supplies ready. Schools and hospitals were major customers for CIR food. CIR food required a system that could perform at an ultra-blazing speed to enable predictive analytics on the budget forecasting and advanced planning for supply chain management. CIR food was earlier running SAP on Unix platform with ERP and business intelligence systems.

Transforming SAP landscape from Unix to SUSE (Software and System Entwicklung) Linux Enterprise server powered by SAP HANA has shown significant cost benefits for CIR food. CIR food has seen cost savings and ROI of 70%. Reports are running 20 minutes earlier producing results now under a second.

Consumer products and food and beverage firms are experiencing similar trends and nuances for business analytics that are in need of algorithms for price elasticity. Maple Leaf Foods is a giant packaged meats organizations in Canada. Maple Leaf revenues were C$4.4 billion CAD in 2013, and C$4.9 billion CAD in 2012. The complexities for perishable packaged foods arise from the short shelf life, freshness of the food, and dynamic weather conditions.

Maple Leaf Foods required an agile system for pricing, and the ability to predict the demand per season. Maple Leaf foods acquired several companies in the recent years; which led to maintaining data across 35 different ERP platforms. The price elasticity and fragmentation of data created increased complexity. LeapFrog was the business transformation workhorse for Maple Leaf Foods. It was a global SAP initiative to consolidate all 35 instances into a single SAP ERP global platform instance and SAP BW for analytics running on Oracle with the traditional disk-storage system.

As the business grew, the data volumes doubled. SAP BW was sourced with Finance, COPA, SAP CRM, and SAP trade promotion management data. The performance of the system was plagued with problems, and reports started to slow down. In 2012, Maple Leaf Foods implemented SAP HANA and achieved the status of first Canadian corporation to go live with SAP HANA in Canada. Maple Leaf foods also powered their SAP BPC system with SAP HANA. The performance was spiked to 1,000 times for some potential business scenarios. The data was standardized, normalized, scrubbed, and sanitized as SAP HANA filtered through all the data attributes reducing redundant database models, which resulted in 25 reports from 500 reports with new data models.

Molson Coors had seven SAP ERP landscape instances and three SAP BW instances for various companies. Ten years ago, SAP BW was implemented. SAP BW receives data from SCM, CRM, HR, and shop floor management, SAP ERP systems with FI-AR (financials accounts receivables), FI-AP (financials accounts payables), COPA, MM (materials management), SD (sales and distribution), IM (inventory management), and PP (production planning) running on multiple SAP instances. As the business operations expanded internationally, Molson Coors acquired a number of systems. BI emerged as their central core system as data feeds were flowing from their spaghetti heterogeneous legacy systems.

The nightly batch jobs were running from 48 to 72 hours. They needed one version of the truth from where they could report from a single data source. For any prototype it took them one to two weeks to build a report from multiple InfoCubes and data sources. Presently, it only takes one day to finish the prototype. For example, a feed from one SAP ERP instance would require changes to six InfoCubes, three extractors, and three DSO (data store objects). The delta load that used to take 20 minutes before SAP HANA implementation, now takes 2 seconds. In the case of data load failure, they have significant time to perform the data load. It now only takes only 5 minutes to reload. BW cube-to-cube loads are now 10 times faster than before. Operational data store (ODS) activations have shown a 70% to 80% reduction in time. The architectural complexity of BI has been dramatically reduced.

SAP HANA implementation has reduced the database size to 900 GB; earlier they had 4.6TB on Oracle system. They implemented SAP HANA on HP server 3+1 nodes with 512GB RAM. Now, they are in SAP BW 7.4.

Frucor, is an Australasian beverages company famous for it is 'V' energy drink and for manufacturing soft drinks. The energy drinks had a humble beginning decades ago. Recently, in 2009, the Japanese company Suntory group bought it (Frucor, 2014). Similar to what Maple Leaf Foods experienced, a series of acquisitions created an increasingly complex architecture of business intelligence systems at Frucor. Frucor has undertaken cloud-based SAP HANA implementation project to power SAP BW, and SAP BPC that had non-Unicode SQL database earlier under 6 weeks. The BW queries accelerated by 100 times, and data loads sped up by 10 times.

According to the co-founder of WeissBeerger, the overall beer industry is worth $500 billion a year. So far, is no significant technology to identify how much beer is served from each tap from the bar, how much has been consumed, and how much is spilled.

WeissBeerger is an alcohol analytical tool that runs on the SAP HANA cloud, which can connect to beer tap and point of sales of the cash register. The data from WeissBeerger flows wirelessly into the SAP HANA cloud and draws the comparisons with analytics between the beer flowing through the tap and revenues generated from the cash register. WeissBeerger powered by SAP HANA has reduced 12% spill of the beer.

Another utility corporation has upgraded their SAP NetWeaver BW 7.3 platforms to SAP HANA. The DSO activation earlier had shown a time of 21 hours and 40 minutes for about 5.2 M records. However, SAP HANA has improved it by 32 times and shown the process completed in less than 40 minutes. The data loads into optimized DSO; optimized SAP HANA InfoCubes have shown an improvement of 2.7 times. The results have shown the data load was complete in 30 minutes as opposed to previous 1 hour 30 minutes of time for 50k+ invoices with 350+ line items. The data compression ratio has incomparably reduced the RDBMS data space from 4.3 TB to 0.73 TB once the data migrated to SAP HANA. The queries performed on aggregated data sets has shown an improvement of 471 times and produced the output in 1 second versus 471 seconds from the earlier run before migrating to SAP HANA.

An automotive industry has upgraded their SAP NetWeaver BW 7.3 and powered by SAP HANA. The optimized SAP HANA InfoCubes have shown speeds by a factor of 1.39 times; DSO activation has shown extreme improvement by 4.15x. When the queries compared from traditional RDBMS SAP NetWeaver BW, it showed an improvement of 8.5x; BW Webi reports were executed faster by 11.6 times. HANA optimized InfoCubes have shown a response time within 45 times; that was faster by 26 times when compared with traditional RDBMS BW system.

A Painless Future with SAP HANA

Seoul's National University Hospital has eight centers established in 1946. It has a pre-establishment history of 150 years as a front-runner of medicine with 21,400 beds and one of the most pioneering hospitals in the world to realize the vision of innovative technologies to reduce the usage of antibiotics. It is recognized as the first hospital in Asia Pacific region to go paperless in 2003, and started obtaining electronic forms from patients via PC. Recently, iPad has been introduced to submit the patient forms electronically. Seoul's National University Hospital went live in 2003 with best-in-class practices recommended by Healthcare Information and Management Systems by adoption of electronic medical records. It built a network of networks that can connect one health insurance provider or hospital to another seamlessly and overcome the patching of incompatible protocols between the systems similar to what the banking industry has achieved in wireless protocols.

This bolstered the Seoul National University Hospital ability to digitize their physical order entry system, business intelligence clinical decision support systems, patient medical records permanent database storage, and electronic prescription systems. It helped building a nationwide single data structure standard to allow the systems to talk to each other seamlessly. The closed loop medication administration was implemented with RFID that scans the barcodes allowed to secure five rights of medication. The five rights are (a) the right time; (b) right route; (c) right drug; (d) right dose, and; (e) right patient. This led to the development of a clinical data warehouse for data analysis of the EMRs (electronic medical record) with ETL processes. The EMR implementation with disaster recovery system led to health information exchange between Seoul's National University and several other clinics.

These clinics were under private ownership for online emergency referrals such as rooms and ambulances. This brought a total of 50 private clinics into the network in Seoul by 2006.

Seoul's National University Hospital initially had suffered some data warehouse system integration issues with the velocity for the extraction of the data. The speed of velocity showed 30 minutes to 1 hour to extract a data range of 3 to 6 months. The data types were too many including free text that was fed into the system by the medical practitioners, which would be hard to use for data analysis. This led to big data issues to tie the data between the free text and the medical image data for reporting and analytics. Korea, being the pioneer of in-memory databases, allowed CIO Hee Hwang to consider SAP HANA, since, 10 years worth of data can be retrieved in 2 to 3 seconds. Unlike the US, Seoul National University Hospital provided third-line antibiotics pre-surgery for 5 to 6 days. US medical associations recommend only 1 to 2 days of 1st line of antibiotics before surgery. The continued use of third-line antibiotics can break the immunization system and resist the viruses, requiring extensive medical care for weeks. SAP HANA reduced the usage of third-line antibiotics from 5.8% to 1.2% and subsequently to no antibiotics with real-time data analytics.

Charité Universitätsmedizin Berlin is the second largest hospital in Europe that has alone produced eight Nobel laureates, with more than half of them in physiology or medicine for Germany. It has also produced 66% of the world's Nobel laureates in medicine (SAP, 2014). It employs more than 12,800 full-time staff that includes scientists and medical practitioners with a history of 300 years. Every year, the hospital treats 127,400 inpatients and 500,000 outpatient cases. In 2010, it experienced a 30% rapid rate of growth with inpatient and outpatient cases, research data, and medical records volume.

Implementation of SAP EMR unwired 2.0 led to a quick diagnosis and analysis of patient records on tablets.

However, the exponential growth of data volumes with clinical research data did not bode well to retrieve 500,000 data elements in each patient. Previously, the researchers and physicians had to take the cues from the notes written with various diagnostic causes by several medical practitioners, and compile that data for each patient from paper-based files. The data was not normalized. The fragmentation of data led to numerous numbers of sources and formats causing increased catastrophic delays especially where productivity was concerned with the data analysis with diminished time on actual cure.

SAP HANA implementation with an increasingly popular SAP EMR mobility application for clinical research led to the elimination of paper-based records and digitalization and normalization of the data. SAP HANA has created 500,000 data points for each patient and quickly stored more than 900 million entries with a single source of information. SAP iPad EMR app has allowed diagnosing the data instantly and providing ad-hoc reporting. Going paperless and getting the data directly into SAP EMR has significantly cut down queue processing times of the patients.

SAP HANA buoyed by electronic medical records, and SAP HANA Oncolyzer headed by SAP Innovation Center in Potsdam, built in collaboration with Charité Institute of Pathology, and Hasso Plattner Institute, has allowed clinical researchers to select the candidates for cancer clinical trials effortlessly with commonly suggested data points. SAP HANA Oncolyzer suggests various types of cancer tumor types, demographic factors, and earlier treatments to prepare the clinical trial. Every time a new DNA type has been added to the columnar DB, the SAP HANA Oncolyzer runs the diagnostics to gather the data from half a million data points.

This aided Charité Universitätsmedizin Berlin to be a unique cancer research facility in the world. It could analyze any external data points connecting to different systems and networks in unstructured, and structured format such as CT (computed tomography) scans, blood samples, X-rays (electromagnetic radiation of short wavelength produced when high-speed electrons strike a solid target between 0.01 to 10 nanometers (3×10^{16} Hz to 3×10^{19} Hz), and any other medical imaging data. SAP HANA on top of the research data has also accelerated financial reporting. It also has accelerated clinical order management, surgery outpatient care systems, operating room management, and improved patient experience.

To create a pain-free future and provide top-notch transcendental patient care, Charité Universitätsmedizin Berlin is breaking new ground with SAP HANA running on some powerful commercial off-the-shelf Intel Xenon X7560 processors. These processors helped to analyze data in excess of 20 TB in just a few seconds. The initial run of the quality system on HP Proliant DL580 G7 with 2 Intel Xeon X7560 running at 2.27GHz (Gigahertz) and 24 MB cache (with eight cores per processor) has proven to be effective. It yielded great results with data retrieval before deploying it on production system. Leveraging the rise of extensive parallelism, Intel HT (hyper-threading) technology aids 16 threads per each socket. This allowed SAP HANA to run on gargantuan volumes of clinical data. This helped make all the calculations and reduce the previous cycle of 6 years of clinical development to introduce a new drug or therapy in healthcare industry, and cut back the risk exposure of discovery time and inaccurate results from clinical trials and pre-development.

SAP released SPS 09 pack in October 2014 for SAP HANA with special integration for IOT and mIOT big data. The new features contain data streaming capabilities to receive various types of data and take action on such millions of events per second. The mIOT devices can be either connected through SAP or to Hadoop. All the high-value data can be streamed into SAP HANA for instant analytics, and the direct data can stay in Hadoop for any historical trend analytics. SAP HANA's Smart Data Access allows parallel processing and analysis of data in both of SAP HANA and Hadoop simultaneously. SAP HANA introduced dynamic tiering can transfer the super-extreme volumes of data from the main memory to disk in columnar-based storage. SAP HANA can schedule a Hadoop map reduce job from HANA and transfer the result set back to SAP HANA from Hadoop distributed file system for performing analysis.

Oracle introduced Exadata in-memory computing with a combination of DRAM and flash memory. The data caching strategy built by Oracle allows it to switch between DRAM and flash memory. Exadata can deliver up to 100 Gb/s from the flash memory, which does not have compression on the data. Oracle Exadata uses hybrid columnar compression, which is a combination of row-based and columnar-based storage. Oracle Exadata with hybrid columnar and flash caching strategy can provide much higher bandwidth. It can cache up to 44 TB of Exadata flash cache in combination with hybrid columnar strategy that compresses the data ratio by 15 to 20 times. However, 26 TB of DRAM and flash in one rack of Exadata machine X-3 could be misleading, as the maximum DRAM memory could go up to 256 GB with no flash memory. Therefore, it is remote memory that is accessed through InfiniBand Network with 40 Gb/s. This does not make it a true in-memory database technology. SAP HANA does not use flash memory and use continuous DRAM memory for in-memory computing. However, it is expensive and requires recommendations with alternative future memory technologies.

The world needs new drugs and therapies to rapidly cure diseases and prevent outbreaks. The rise of MIOT is likely to generate massive volumes of medical data in the next five years. This helps tracking and monitoring the health apart from the medical devices that generate such data at hospitals. Gartner stated the Internet of Things is expected to spark technology diffusion in creating 100 billion IOT devices by 2020. This is estimated to be 75 billion by Morgan Stanley.

The mIOT devices are useful for simple health monitoring, medical imaging, and surgical systems that generate heavy medical data, with a significant input of patient data, prior demographics, and clinical medical data. DLR's (Deutsche Luft-Reederei) Institute of Robotics and Mechatronics has introduced digital tele-presence of the remote physicians. This is to perform minimally invasive robotic heart surgeries with the aid of three interconnected robots. The surgical data is on the leading edge with the big data wave with monumental database volumes, heterogeneously structured, and unstructured data types integrated with EMRs. Thirty percent of the world's big data medical and surgical data is generated from healthcare industry.

Global monitoring of the global pulse in real-time can prevent and demarcate the dynamic demands of disease outbreaks. In a connected cloud world of Internet of Everything, the right analysis IMDB tool such as SAP HANA on right data flowing from mIOTs from the world can provide the source of epidemics of viruses. It can act at the right time to contain the outbreaks for the rest of the territories and countries. The increased global connectivity can converge the machine-generated data by big data tools embedded in mIOTs. It can combine with human-created data connected to the Internet to build a cloud-based global pharmaceutical store that is capable of connecting to any other drug store in the world to provide the availability of the inventory of medicines, vaccines, and blood. A cloud-based center for disease control and prevention can connect to any other center in the world and sift through the trends for prevention. SAP HANA Oncolyzer has already proved creating and combining half a million data points can pull up similar genetic profiles from the system creating recommendations to treat a lymphoma patient.

The traditional research and development costs for each pharmaceutical company are looming large on the horizon. The conglomeration of top 20 pharmaceutical companies in the world has driven the product proliferation of big pharma to remove the longstanding roadblocks of research and development costs. The mountain of data flowing from big pharma clinical trails can push forward a new wave of big data movement that can reinforce anonymous clinical trails data and genetic profiles to support global pharmaceutical companies for their research in introducing new products.

The healthcare industry spends $150 billion every year on research and development costs to introduce new drugs into the market. According to McKinsey & Co. Inc., a global management-consulting firm, big data tools can reduce the research and clinical development by $40 billion to $70 billion.

Data is not useful without information. SAS Institute from North Carolina launched an initiative with SAS In-database and SAS High-performance analytics software. It has built a private cloud to store such big data from clinical trials for co-innovation between all big pharma companies who can access the data from the private cloud and reduce the research time for product development. GlaxoSmithKline is one of the first companies that joined this initiative to contribute the big data from clinical trials followed by Sanofi, Viiv Healthcare, Roche, and Novartis.

Collaborating with SAS for GlaxoSmithKline in building a private cloud has moved one of the largest indicators in big data movement for the healthcare industry. This program opened the gateway for global pharmaceutical companies for co-innovation. However, conventional wisdom suggests that GlaxoSmithKline could have driven their corporate strategy to integrate all their project sites with SAP HANA Enterprise private cloud for elasticity, flexibility, increased global connectivity, integration, and high-performance analytics. GlaxoSmithKline could have run their entire SAP Business Suite, SAP NetWeaver BW, and SAP big data tools on SAP HANA Enterprise cloud to support the language, currency, and financial requirements to increase enterprise-wide agility.

GlaxoSmithKline has an existing footprint of SAP IS-Pharmaceuticals ERP, SAP HR, SAP BW, and SAP SCM with 17,000 users with the presence in 31 countries and 67 sites. With such a colossal footprint of SAP, the integration with SAP HANA Enterprise cloud would make sense for sustainability and future roadmaps for standardizing the data management models, and master data governance combining Apache Hadoop + R language integration + SAP HANA native integration. Sanofi Pasteur, Viiv Healthcare, Hoffmann-La Roche, and Novartis International AG are one of the front-loaded implementers of SAP IS-Pharmaceuticals (industrial solutions), who could seamlessly integrate with SAP HANA Enterprise cloud.

R language has some rich computational capabilities with visualization tools, data mining built-in techniques, and native integration with Apache Hadoop and SAP HANA. SAP HANA fully supports R integration with either RODBC (open database connectivity for R language) driver or RServe. R has proven to be the best language integrated with SAP HANA in a cloud-based environment. The downside of GlaxoSmithKline's selection with SAS-In-database is lack of integration with ERP R&D, EMR, ERP IS-P (industrial solutions for pharmaceuticals), CRM, and SRM for the organization with high scalability, back up, and restore mechanisms.

SAP HANA has been the go-to in-memory database engine. SAP HANA can support all the heterogeneous needs by integrating with R language for statistical analysis, modeling, clustering, predictive modeling, visualization, and native integration of an organization's Enterprise Information Systems to connect. GlaxoSmithKline should create its own SAP HANA Enterprise private cloud. They should take the ownership of the global pharmaceutical initiative to collaborate with big pharma companies to run their genome sequencing analysis and cancer research to structure and bring all big pharma research and development units under a single roof. When SAP HANA-SAS pharma architecture prevails, and HANA powers SAS, big pharma industries significantly benefit by re-platforming from SAS private cloud to SAP HANA Enterprise private cloud. Current targeted industries for SAS applications powered by HANA include financial services, telecommunications, retail, consumer products, and manufacturing.

The data is half equation without information in information systems. There are 3.2 billion pairs of As, Cs, Gs, and Ts in a DNA of human body known as amino acid base pairs, and they do have a sequence in a genome just like the binary data stored in a computer machines. Decoding the evolution of the human genome in chunks with parallelism and reassembling can aid medical researchers to identify specific genes.

The human genome project was launched by US companies in 1990 and was complete in 2003 after analysis and synthesis of the information from 3.2 billion DNA pairs in the human genetic blueprint that are the building blocks for human life. This has revolutionized the healthcare industry. There is still some research to be performed on various patient's DNA code to understand the genesis of diseases, mutations, and variations of tumor cells. Genomics England, in collaboration with the UK Department of Health, and the San Diego based company Illumina is launching another project to study 100,000 genomes to understand cell growth patterns and rare diseases.

Mitsui Knowledge Industry, a Tokyo based bioinformatics company has implemented SAP HANA to perform genome-sequencing analysis on 3.2 billion DNA base pairs distributed across 23 chromosome pairs in the human genome. The initial analysis has finished in 20 minutes (SAP, 2014). Approximately 30,000 genes in the human genome create an average of three proteins. The traditional RDBMS and SAP HANA IMDB have shown a difference of speed by 400,000 times with native R Integration. It is used as a data mining technique that works internally with columnar storage and an open source language, which is license free and can perform some visualization dashboards on screening of cancer tumor cells up to 80TB of data. Apache Hadoop acts as high-speed storage of the initial genome data uploaded for data pre-processing into SAP HANA. SAP HANA security concept also allows performing cross-analysis between global pharmaceutical companies without having actually to exchange the confidential patient data from clinical trials.

Apache Hadoop with RLANG (R language) can convert the data types, and SAP HANA IMDB can store, and calculate, and perform analytics on the data once transformed into data frames for HANA IMDB columnar data store. The future state of big pharma is to pioneer the frontier of the healthcare industry in defining disease stages, performing genome sequencing analytics, and proteome to understand the map of the genetic profiles for identifying the origin of cancer tumor cell disintegration and ability to reverse such fragmentation.

Technische Universität München in collaboration with SAP SE (Societas Europaea) Innovation center launched a research proteome initiative. Proteomics DB is a columnar database powered by SAP HANA to analyze proteins in over 18,000 human genes that make up 90% of the human proteome. The detection of proteins in specific genes can revolutionize new drug development to target specific genomes in human and exclude proteome areas, thus removing any side effects that can cause problems to humans. SAP HANA has created more than 160 million data points for each 2.4GB worth of proteome sample for 3.7TB raw proteome data stored in ProteomicsDB. ProteomicsDB has been released for medical institutions as a public database for medical research purposes.

The deluge of big data in healthcare industry has created unprecedented growth of medical records in everyday life. Each genome created 800MB of data in the clinics. Each clinic creates approximately 50GB of healthcare Information systems data. Currently, the global healthcare industry has data of 15+PB of human genomes. The medical prescription transaction data in the pharmacies has more than 100GB of data and is growing. Any scan performed by medical devices on humans produces 10GB of data.

The medical devices industry has experienced a growth of 8% year-to-year from 2001. The medical devices industry has experienced a compound annual growth rate (CAGR) of 9% year-to-year from 2001. The revenues generated from medical devices doubled from $74 billion to $148 billion from 2001 to 2009. An adverse report with quality risks in medical devices released by the Federal

Drug Administration (FDA) has shown 60% of surgical devices have quality defects from 2005 through 2009. The defects ranged from product design to quality control of the manufacturing with a CAGR of 15%. The patients injured from medical devices increased the number of 7,000 to 28,000 between 2001 and 2009. The medical devices recall CAGR rate registered at 6% from 2003 to 2009. A research report from iData Research suggests a forecasted growth of CAGR of 10% for neurological medical device makers for the market leaders Medtronic, Boston Scientific, and St. Jude Medical. Boston Scientific has implemented SAP HANA with mobility with more than 4,500 iPads; thus, SAP HANA has shown a performance improvement of 3,600 times.

Johnson and Johnson, Siemens Healthcare, GE Healthcare, Medtronic Inc., and Baxter International are ranked among the top five medical device companies by revenues for 2013. The information explosion of complaints from medical institutions and patients about medical devices has grown exponentially in the last decade. Medical device makers such as Medtronic with a global presence in 140 countries and 280 project sites capturse the complaints and returns on SAP CRM and the medical devices in real-time to send to field agents via a modern mobile device connectivity such as SAP mobile platform (SAP SMP), the service manager mobile solution for service orders, service confirmations, and efficient handling of SAP CRM complaints and returns management.

This allowed Medtronic to respond to the FDA, customers, and medical institutions at a rapid speed to keep up the competitive advantage of medical devices with Boston Scientific and St. Jude. Most of the complaints were received in the large text objects format, and some of them had product solutions from Medtronic. However, Medtronic's legacy data warehousing system could not handle such huge volumes of text. It could not perform analytics on both structured and unstructured text types that contain a complaint and provide a resolution, which delayed the solution by weeks. Medtronic has chosen to implement SAP BW on SAP HANA. Medtronic has strategized loading data into the SAP BW system from various systems including SAP CRM, and transformation is performed with SAP Data Services, and then subsequently, data has been pushed down to SAP HANA. This has boosted the SAP BOBJ report out in 3 minutes from earlier legacy system of 3 hours.

According to a survey held by TechAmerica Foundation, 83% of Federal IT officials have stated approximately $380 billion of federal budget can be saved by leveraging big data tools. The City of Boston has implemented SAP HANA for government administration and performance. Now, city of Boston citizens can review problematic properties in the neighborhood with SAP HANA mobile application. The calls made to the city of Boston for enquiring about problematic properties was reduced by 66%. CitizenInsight free mobile app can provide continuous access around-the-clock to all the citizens of Boston. The licensing permits for building can access data in a few seconds. The administration can monitor 911 calls and incidents in the neighborhood. This enabled the city to extract the data with blazing speed and improve the efficiency of their systems as well as reduce the crime rate by 55%. The implementation of SAP HANA has led to a reduction of pending city permits to 10 from 600 instantly. The government administration can now track 18 new performance scorecards from different departments of the city at one time.

Rock Hill, a city in South Carolina, implemented CitizenInsight Mobile app for government performance, and the city administration is powered by SAP HANA. The State of Indiana is implementing SAP HANA for strategic management and government performance.

The world needs more reconnaissance applications, which are command control applications that can run at blazing speed. In the Southwest US, a plane grounded just for few hours' costs them $4 million. DHL (Dalsey, Hillblom & Lynn) reported a cargo plane grounded for a single day costs nearly $1 million. SAP HANA has rapidly added solutions to SAP for aerospace and defense solutions in 2013. The expanded SAP aerospace and defense solution will aid original equipment manufacturers (OEMs) to gain insights into real-time equipment status to provide rapid response to customer requests. SAP HANA also bolsters the engine manufacturers for real-time *on-wing* data with real-time predictive analytics.

Honeywell Aerospace generates $10 billion in annual revenues delivering both commercial and defense engines and avionics. SAP HANA powers aerospace and defense companies to analyze the tsunami of performance data, sensor data, for the Department of Defense (DOD), and command, control, communications, computers, intelligence, surveillance, and reconnaissance (C4ISR) applications. Earlier, Honeywell Aerospace was leveraging SAP BOBJ 3.0 with Oracle DB that took 12 hours for extracting 5 TB of data. SAP HANA now powers Honeywell Aerospace in 14 weeks operating in over 80 global project sites for COPA, financials, and order management functionality, resulting in retrieving the same data in the near-real time of a few seconds. The implementation scope included SAP HANA, SAP BOBJ 4.0, SLT (SAP landscape transformation), and BODS.

Sagem, an aerospace company from France, has powered their SAP NetWeaver BW platform by SAP HANA. This has resulted in rapid response to the execution of queries and improved the response time by 97%; on a given test scenario it was improved from 112 seconds to 7 seconds. The database has been compressed by 206% from 2.15TB to 443 GB. The database loads have increased from 531 seconds to 231 seconds. The activation of the data has been decreased by 94.1% from 699 seconds to 41 seconds. The cache has been sped up by 98% and reduced from 135 seconds to 3 seconds.

Liquid rocket prolusion technology has evolved and come a long way from Atlas I to Atlas V and Delta I to Delta IV family. Lockheed Martin, founded in 1995, is one of the largest aerospace companies in the US. In 2005, Boeing and Lockheed Martin collaborated to create a 50-50 joint venture called United Launch Alliance. It was to launch US Boeing Delta and Atlas rockets in partnership with US Evolved Expendable Launch Vehicle program. Recently, Lockheed Martin built algorithms on SAP HANA(R) platform by performing predictive analytics on historical trends and procurement times for materials before they infuse into the life cycle of supply chain management. This allowed Lockheed Martin to improve the predictive accuracy of pricing and lead-time estimates for the goods.

Qualitative Results

The qualitative results are based on large-scale and highly structured surveys conducted by IDC and empirical data from unbiased interviews conducted directly by SAP with their customers. The customers include information technology directors, information technology managers, business managers, business analysts, SAP HANA architects, and systems analysts from various industries. The qualitative results focused on examining the challenges in business that stem from performance and information delays and time for data movement between the OLTP system and the OLAP system. SAP HANA is one of the pioneering in-memory database platforms that thousands of customers adopted as early as 2011, even before Gartner identified it in the trough of disillusionment in 2012.

Research Question 1

SAP innovation center for SAP HANA partner Hasso Plattner Institute wrote a research paper in 2009 on the architecture and possibilities of building a blended database management system that can embed OLAP and OLTP on the same platform. This led to a prototype of a solution with a German brewery company to diffuse SAP HANA in-memory database technology. The prototype components included 5 years worth of SAP financial data. The results have shown that, when row-based tabular data has been compressed to columnar-based data, the table was compressed from 35GB to 8GB. The performance improvement was factored in between 100 to 1,000.

SAP was the first organization in the world to implement first-generation of SAP HANA in-memory database technology in 2010. SAP HANA implementation compressed database size for SAP from 7.1TB to 1.8TB. SAP innovation center in Potsdam partnered with Hasso Plattner Institute, and the Charité Institute of Pathology has built SAP HANA Oncolyzer. Per SAP, SAP HANA was the fastest product to diffuse big data and in-memory database platforms to several customers through awareness, interest, trial, and adoption to-date. SAP HANA gained strong momentum so through end of 2014, and was able to implement SAP HANA for more than 5,800 global customers and 1,850 SAP Business Suites powered by SAP HANA implementations.

In a research survey conducted by IDC on behalf of SAP with 352 participants, the speed, accuracy, and granularity of the data were the main concerns for business intelligence. SAP, in collaboration with IDC, conducted surveys using business intelligence to disseminate big data awareness, interest, evaluation, trial, and adoption. The results have shown that 40% of the survey respondents were spending more than 48 hours to close their financial statements. In addition, 25% of the respondents experienced extreme information delays with the current architecture of RDBMS based business intelligence solutions. The employees spent 70% of their time for data movement between OLTP to OLAP through RDBMS system. Four hundred information technology managers participated in yet another survey conducted by IDC Results revealed that the data migration took 24 hours roughly in 50% of the cases on a single platform. The migration of the data from one transactional platform to another business intelligence platform has taken approximately 48 hours for the rest of the 50% of the cases. The information delay due to the waiting has increased from 1 week to 7 days.

SAP sponsored IDC to conduct another research survey to speed up the interest of SAP HANA and evaluate the heterogeneous environments with fragmented database systems. With this, SAP wants to diffuse the adoption of SAP HANA providing a trial version for up to 30 days. Their survey revealed that 35% of the respondents rated satisfaction with four stars. Results also revealed that 30% of the respondents found it takes 2 days to complete an operational build of report. In addition, 40% of the respondents indicated that their current business intelligence systems were not capable of performing predictive analytics, simulations, or real-time visibility of the data. These surveys were beneficial in answering the research question to speed up the diffusion of SAP HANA product to various entities by building critical business objectives for the product releases in multiple phases and resolving the challenges.

An early survey in 2012 conducted by SAP at SAP Slovenia and Croatia Innovations event has shown that an early adopter of SAP HANA, Asian Paints, has achieved data compression ratio of 6:1 with respect to RDBMS disk-based system. The performance time of query execution has improved by a range of 15 to 255 times. The data load time was reduced by 95%. Another early adopter of SAP HANA, Yazaki a global automotive parts supplier, was able to accelerate their finance and controlling processes. Southern California Edison has shown an improvement of 5 times after SAP HANA implementation, as opposed to early RDBMS implementation. Their SAP CRM system powered by SAP HANA demonstrated 75% performance improvement in UI. SAP CRM database compression has shown an improvement of 7.5 times. Another early adopter of SAP HANA, Lenovo, significantly improved their reporting by 20 times. The database compression improved by 2 times. SAP BW query performance improved by 60 times bringing the query time from hours to seconds.

T-mobile has shown an improvement of ROI with the results of $10 to $25 savings as a win-back strategy on customer subscription services. Earlier RDBMS system was running the analysis report forn over a week to scan 2 billion records for over 2 million customers. SAP HANA has reduced the time of 1 week to hours to complete the analysis. This is an improvement by 56 times. Provimi, a consumer based product company, has implemented SAP HANA to power their SAP ERP COPA solution. The capital reduction showed 500,000 euros during the first week. The monthly closing activities were improved by 40%. Overall analytics were improved by 15,000 times.

The early adopters of SAP HANA such as Mitsui Knowledge Industry implemented SAP HANA and improved the analysis of cancer DNA by performing human genome sequencing on 3.2 billion DNA base pairs in 20 minutes as opposed to their earlier run time of 3 days time, an improvement of 216 times. Another early adopter of SAP HANA, Charite information systems of Charité Universitätsmedizin Berlin, has analyzed 300 million records in 5 seconds. Cisco, a high tech company, implemented SAP HANA and results were amazing. Cisco was able to complete the season analysis of purchasing patterns in 2 to 10 seconds. The University of Kentucky was the first university in the world to implement in-memory based database technology SAP HANA. The University of Kentucky has around 28,000 students on average. Earlier, the University of Kentucky was running the analysis of graduation retention rates through a disk-based RDBMS database system. In the IDC research survey, University of Kentucky showed $6.7 million savings over a period of 5 years with an ROI of 509%. This has ignited in-memory database adoption awareness in the public service sector. The reporting was accelerated by 420 times, and data loads improved by 15 times. The data compression ratio was 77% over traditional RDBMS before SAP HANA implementation. The time for data movement between OLAP and OLTP improved by 87%. The database updates and reporting times improved by 80%.

Consumer products and beverages industries joined the big data movement as early as 2011. Red Bull was one of the frontrunners of SAP HANA implementation. Database size was 1.5 TB before SAP implementation; the database compressed to 0.3 TB after SAP HANA implementation. CIR Foods SAP implementation has improved the ROI by 70%. Reporting times were improved, and results were produced under a second as opposed to an earlier run time of 20 minutes. Maple Leaf Foods was the first Canadian corporation to implement SAP HANA. The overall performance spiked up to 1,000 times as opposed to the traditional RDBMS disk-based system. Molson Coors has improved prototype times from 2 weeks to 1 day after SAP HAPA implementation. ODS activation time was improved by 70% to 80%. Oracle database size of 4.6 TB reduced to 900 GB (Theroux-Benoni & Moerski, 2014). Frucor, an Australasian beverages company, improved BW query execution time by 100 times. WeissBeerger, an alcoholic analytics company, implemented SAP HANA on enterprise cloud and saved the beer spill by 12%.

A utility company was able to improve the database size from 4.3 TB to 0.73 TB. DSO activation was improved by 32 times. Data loads improved by 2.7 times. Queries on aggregated data sets had shown an improvement of 471 times. An automotive company implemented SAP HANA. The data loads improved by 1.39 times. DSO activation improved by 4.15 times. Reporting times increased by 11.6 times. InfoCubes response time increased by 45 times.

Seoul's National University Hospital was the first hospital in Asia Pacific region to implement in-memory database technology SAP HANA. The data extraction speed was 30 minutes to 1 hour before SAP HANA implementation for a date range of 3 to 6 months. After SAP HANA implementation, the data was extracted in 2 to 3 seconds for a date range of 10 years. Seoul National University Hospital, for safety purposes, provides third-line antibiotics pre-surgery for 5 to 6 days due to lack of real-time data analytics. US medical associations recommend only 1 to 2 days of first line antibiotics before surgery. The continued usage of third-line antibiotics can break the immunization system and resist viruses, requiring extensive medical care for weeks. SAP HANA reduced the usage of third-line antibiotics from 5.8% to 1.2% and subsequently to no antibiotics with real-time data analytics.

Earlier adopter of SAP HANA includes the hospital, Charité Universitätsmedizin Berlin. Charité Universitätsmedizin Berlin retrieved data of 20 TB in few seconds for analytics purposes. Technische Universität München partnered with SAP innovation center and launched a proteome research project. ProteomicsDB is a columnar database powered by SAP HANA for analyzing 18,000 human genes that are responsible for the human proteome. SAP HANA took the baseline of 3.7 TB raw proteome data stored in ProteomicsDB and created 160 million data points for a refined sample of 2.4 GB.

In public services sector, according to the research conducted by TechAmerica Foundation, implementing big data solutions can save $380 billion of budget. The city of Boston was a pioneering government sector to implement SAP HANA by developing an application titled CitizenInsight that can expedite the processing of license permits for properties and 911 call monitoring. This reduced the crime rate by 55%. The pending license permits for properties were reduced to 10 from 600 instantly. The city of Boston can now track 18 performance scorecards that are part of different departments of the city (Quirk, n.d.). Rockhill followed the city of Boston.

SAP HANA has made some pioneering advances into the aerospace industry with its in-memory database technology. SAP HANA powered Honeywell Aerospace with SAP HANA, SAP BOBJ 4.0, and SAP BODS. Sagem, a French aerospace company, has powered its SAP BW platform by SAP HANA. The query response time increased by 97% from 112 seconds to 7 seconds. The compression ratio on database was 206%. The database reduced from 2.15 TB to 443 TB. The database loads time reduced from 531 seconds to 231 seconds. The activation of data accelerated from 641 seconds to 41 seconds. Lockheed Martin implemented SAP HANA with R language with predictive analytics for performing historical and trending analysis for supply chain management.

Research Question 2

SAP HANA has been the apostle of the movement by entering the foray of big data, in-memory database technology, blended database management system with OLTP and OLAP and measuring the results against several RDBMS big data adopters with disk-based memory systems. SAP HANA has shown that it can scan the database for database entries at 3 MB/s per each core on a multi-core-80-core server. The speed for each node was evaluated at 250

GB/s. The INSERT database operations have shown 1.5 million inserts per second or 120 million records per second on each node. Database aggregation on SAP HANA, has shown a speed of 12 million records per second, or 960 million records per node. This has shown a vivid performance difference of 100 times over disk-based database systems.

SAP HANA also has shown the ability to have the blended OLAP and OLTP on a single database system by saving the transaction and automatically populating the content for business intelligence reporting purposes. Many of the other big data appliances have challenges to blend the database systems for both OLAP and OLTP that have proved to be rigid. Moreover, 21% of the respondents of a research survey conducted by IDC responded that it is a complex challenge for business to move data manually between OLAP and OLTP. Oracle has a hybrid row-based, columnar-based in-memory database. IBM DB2 Blu acceleration has column-based storage, however, lacks the big data enterprise-ready solution to connect and transfer big data.

Many of the early adopters of other big data appliances have encountered problems of lack of native integration with SAP BW. SAP HANA native integration of SAP BW has shown that SAP HANA can handle the data conversions and data migration challenges with Business Objects Data Services (SAP BODS). SAP HANA has shown that it can run self-service BI reports when SAP BW is powered by SAP HANA on Webi, BEx, and Xcelsius reporting tools. SAP HANA also has shown that the security authorization concept is natively built and can be easily controlled by including corporate-wide security concepts and integration of SAP NetWeaver IDM (identify management).

The main in-memory computing database technologies of IBM, Oracle, and SAP HANA compete in the market. IBM has divided the strategy of in-memory database technology and big data appliance. IBM DB2 Blu acceleration is the in-memory database technology that is based on columnar-based storage. IBM's PureData is a big data appliance for processing super-extreme volumes of data. Oracle runs Exadata on hybrid memory such as flash and DRAM with hybrid columnar-based memory with row-based storage. Oracle Exadata has industrial algorithms for database operations; however, they do not scale up to IBM DB2 Blu acceleration in-memory database industrial algorithms. SAP HANA is the only solution that is big data and enterprise-ready with columnar-based solution.

Research Question 3

mIOT devices that can revolutionize information technology in healthcare industry, speech-to-speech translation, and future memory technologies, keeping in view the economies of flash that are emerging growth technologies. According to an estimate by Gartner, mIOT devices will power 100 billion devices by 2020. In a separate study conducted by Morgan Stanley, the growth of mIOT is estimated at $75 billion. SAP HANA SPS 09 released in October 2014 directly supports streaming medical data and clinical medical data coming through IOT. The global healthcare industry spends around $150 billion every year to introduce a new drug into the market. According to the research conducted by McKinsey Inc., the cost of big data tools development can be reduced to $70 billion.

GlaxoSmithKline has collaborated with SAS to build a private cloud for co-innovation among big pharma companies for clinical trial development. This is a potential area for SAP HANA with Hadoop and R language integration to shape the future of big pharma companies by building a private enterprise cloud for co-innovation among big pharma companies. The future state of SAP HANA is to introduce a smart access platform by integrating big pharma companies under an enterprise private cloud to define disease stages and perform proteome analysis.

The main features of future memory solutions consist of power consumption, cost, time to market, density, scaling, and performance. NAND (Not AND), 3D NAND (Three dimensional negative and) PCRAM (Phase-change memory), STT-RAM (Spin-transfer torque random access memory), and ReRAM (Resistive random-access memory) are the future memory alternatives to DRAM (Dynamic random access memory). The alternative of using DDP (dual die package) and TSV (through-silicon via) in DRAM have cost ramifications. TSV has a projected cost value 22% higher than DDP.

Gartner has identified speech-to-speech translation as one of the *nexus of forces* in the hype cycle for emerging technologies. SAP HANA has potential opportunities to enter the foray of speech-to-speech translation technologies on the CRM platform. SAP HANA has shown potential performance improvements on SAP CRM platform with CTI and IVR integration by 10 times. SAP CRM Web UI has shown an improvement in the performance by 115 times. Search capabilities on inbox have shown 100% improvement. SAP CRM loyalty management has shown 10 times improvement.

Summary

This paper was an examination of how SAP HANA can resolve the biggest conundrums in various industries with awareness, adoption, interest, trial, and evaluation. New independent research analysis was buoyed by empirical data from the surveys conducted by the IDC on behalf of SAP and independent empirical data gathered from the interviews conducted by SAP directly with their customers. The SAP innovation center partnered with Hasso Plattner Institute to build a blended database management in-memory technology that can embed both OLAP and OLTP on a single database system. Both SAP and Hasso Plattner prototyped an in-memory database technology solution with a German brewery solution. The database was compressed from 35 GB to 8 GB. SAP had commercial success to implement SAP HANA for SAP. The database was reduced from 7.1 TB to 1.8 TB.

SAP hopes to bring awareness to the healthcare industry. In the entire history of SAP, SAP HANA has been the fastest product to diffuse big data and in-memory database platforms to several customers through awareness, interest, trial, and adoption to date. SAP HANA gained stronger momentum through end of 2014 and was able to implement SAP HANA for more than 5,800 global customers, and 1,850 SAP Business Suite powered by SAP HANA implementations. According to a research report from Forrester Research Inc., SAP HANA was implemented for 7200 organizations to bring competitive advantage to their firms. SAP HANA Cloud has seen a massive adoption of 1500 corporations by August 2015.

Asian Paints, Yazaki, Southern California Edison, T-Mobile, Provimi, Mitsui Knowledge Industry, Charité Universitätsmedizin Berlin, Cisco, and the University of Kentucky were the first adopters of the SAP HANA product. SAP created a new wave of awareness for consumer products and beverages industries such as Red Bull, CIR Foods, Maple Leaf Foods, and Molson Coors with SAP HANA implementations. Automotive, healthcare, utilities, aerospace, public sector, and government services were other industries adopting SAP HANA.

SAP HANA has the edge with big data appliance capabilities to natively integrate with Apache Hadoop and other big data tools, and it is an enterprise-ready solution to power existing BW solutions or by creating a new business intelligence solution from the ground up.

However, competitors like IBM have divided the strategy and offer two separate solutions for big data and columnar-storage by offering PureData and IBM DB2 Blu acceleration with some powerful industrial algorithms. Oracle offered hybrid memory and hybrid columnar compression leaving limitations to transfer the data from flash memory to main-memory through InfiniBand Network consuming bandwidth. Thus, SAP HANA proved to be an efficient solution that is big data and enterprise solution ready with columnar-storage. However, SAP HANA runs on DRAM memory. It can run on up to 100 TB data of DRAM, but the cost of DRAM memory is expensive. SAP HANA, as an emerging growth technology, should embrace future memory technologies to disseminate the product further into organizations. SAP HANA SPS 09 release in October 2014 offered promising smart data access and data streaming capabilities for enabling integration with IOT and mIOT devices. Gartner predicted speech-to-speech translation and complex event processing as the potential technologies for the next 5 to7 years. SAP HANA has potential opportunities to shift the gears towards these technologies by examining various memory alternative options.

5

Summary, Conclusions, and Recommendations

THE PURPOSE OF the study was to examine big data tools for industrial applications such as SAP HANA, IBM DB2 with Blu acceleration, Apache Cassandra, DataStax, MongoDB, and Oracle Exalytics. This study included a discussion of at disk-based RDBMS databases and an exploration of the advantages of giving a forklift upgrade to in-memory database, which resolves several business conundrums to improve the ROI and reduce the TCO for organizations. The study also was an examination of the trends in future memory technologies such as NAND, 3D NAND, PCRAM, STT-RAM, ReRAM and their cost impacts on database technologies. The future emerging growth technologies such as mIOT, speech-to-speech translation, and complex event processing with neural network type of algorithms to perform parallel processing of the events and data was also discussed.

Summary

Research on conventional RDBMS databases, NoSQL big data tools, and in-memory databases such as SAP HANA was conducted. SAP

HANA supports integration of multiple SAP enterprise platforms such as ERP, CRM, SRM, PPM, PLM, SCM, and FSCM. SAP HANA has polymorphic attributes. SAP HANA allows building a transformation plan and schema dynamically at run time. Thus, data flattening can occur from the analytic view by assembling data from multiple dimensions. SAP HANA stores the data with star schema in a flattened fashion providing a blazing ultra-fast boost to the system for data loads.

The big data market is expected to have projected revenues of $46 billion by 2018. Gartner Inc. has defined big data mainly with four characteristics that are volume, velocity, variety, and veracity. Big data is an up and coming trend. SAP HANA is leading the management charge with in-memory databases. Organizations cannot make decisions when the data extraction takes long times to evolve from heterogeneous systems due to dirty data.

Global NoSQL database tools were reviewed. The global online population has created 90% of the world's big data in the last 2 years. Current RDBMS tools in the world are not efficient to process such super-extreme big data. RDBMS tools have fixed data types for handling the data. NoSQL database tools can handle structured and unstructured data types. NoSQL database architecture is dynamic and schemaless. Most of the NoSQL database tools use JSON document format. JSON format sorts and stores data of hundreds of tables in columns. Unlike RDBMS database, tools require high-scalable servers, unlike NoSQL database tools that can process data with distributed cluster servers. In-memory computing database tools run the data in-memory. RDBMS database tools require multiple server trips for data extraction, updates, delete and insert update operations.

Google Dremel is a big data analytics tool built by Google. Google built Dremel to gain insights on the products released by Google to the world. Google also released an external big data tool, Google BigQuery, for organizations that require analysis of their big data.

While Dremel can process the data for Google Corporation, Google BigQuery can perform analytics for non-Google organizations on the Google proprietary databases such as Gmail, YouTube, Google Docs, and Google Searches. Tokyo Cabinet is a NoSQL database tool written in C language. Tokyo Cabinet has high compression algorithms to reduce the database size. Tokyo Cabinet spawns multiple threads when a search query is triggered to promote the parallelism.

Redis is open-source database software tool written in C language. It works similar to Tokyo Cabinet NoSQL database tool. However, Redis does not support a parallelism concept. MongoDB is a start-up company funded by the CIA, and is written in C language. MongoDB is an open-source-software NoSQL database tool with auto-sharing capabilities. Talend is another open-source software NoSQL database tool, built on the Java platform. Talend runs on top of native Apache Hadoop platform with integration capabilities to connect to SAP HANA. Talend is heavily utilized for master data management and master data governance. Apache Cassandra is a NoSQL database tool written on the Java platform primarily leveraged for social media platforms.

The problem of high-speed big data has been rapidly growing for the last few years. The cost of managing the big data is high. However the expected industrial insights are minimum with RDBMS database tools. This limits the ability of organizations looking to integrate ERP systems with big data with near real-time analytics to gain needed insights. Organizations need to consider in-memory computing database tools such as SAP HANA that are built with a mindset to integrate ERP, CRM, SCM, FSCM, PLM, PPM, and SRM systems. However, organizations face challenges to choose the right in-memory computing database analytics tool to aid their business with predictive analytics for future demand forecasting. Oracle launched Oracle TimesTen and Exadata in-memory database with big data analytics solutions. IBM launched IBM PureData for big data analytics. IBM DB2 BLU acceleration solution is an in-memory database solution offered by IBM with columnar storage and high-compression algorithm techniques.

IBM PureData launched with cloud-computing capabilities as a SaaS solution to integrate software and hardware. IBM acquired Aspera that can perform super-extreme-speed file transfer from cloud to cloud with fasp protocol. IBM DB2 BLU acceleration can integrate SAP applications. However, it is not truly an enterprise and big data solution, as it cannot integrate with Apache Hadoop platform. IBM PureData can integrate with Apache Hadoop platform. This makes it complicated for enterprises that are looking to run a single enterprise and big data ready solution. Oracle Exadata is a software and hardware-integrated solution. However, Oracle Exadata is not a true columnar storage in-memory database. Oracle Exadata uses hybrid columnar compression technology that combines both columnar and row storage techniques.

This present study was focused on the objective of performing analysis on SAP HANA performance benchmarks for various industries such as aerospace, automotive, consumer products, food and beverages, government, healthcare, and utilities. The research focused on the evolution of the big data movement, and how in-memory database computing will shape the future. Results show how SAP HANA aids organizations to diffuse big data with awareness, adoption, interest, trial, and evaluation, and how SAP HANA is better than early big data adopters trying to integrate SAP enterprise applications. McKinsey Global Institute independent research predicted that the GDP of US would rise from 0.8% to 1.7% by 2020. The retail and manufacturing industry powered by big data analytics will add revenues of $325 billion to GDP. In research conducted by IDC, the world's big data is expected to rise by 40,000 exabytes by 2020.

IBM's Aspera *fasp* protocol can transfer data at 24 GB in 30 seconds. Big data is expected to save $100 to $190 billion dollars in healthcare industry. Big data analytics can save $90 billion in the government sector. SAP HANA can partner with 1 hardware vendors to provide the infrastructure and hardware needed to run SAP HANA in enterprise applications. Various hardware configurations to run SAP HANA were reviewed. The IBM DB2 BLU acceleration solution for enterprise applications was reviewed. CenturyLink is an alternative solution for hosting SAP HANA on the cloud environment.

Co-location is another option for hosting SAP HANA solutions. According to IMS research Inc., by 2017, the market for co-location is expected to increase by $10 billion. Cisco Systems has conducted an independent research on cloud traffic data. The research revealed that the cloud traffic will grow by 5.3 ZB from 1.2 ZB by 2017. Global Industry Analytics firm has estimated that the cloud computing service market will increase to $127 billion by 2017.

CenturyLink has performed ROI analysis on SAP HANA both on premise and cloud-hosted environments. The study revealed that a hosted SAP platform costs around $179,000 as opposed to $261,000 with on premise option over a period of 3 years. The ROI has shown that it provides an $81,000 savings for 256GB database. HP provides disaster tolerant solutions for hosting SAP HANA.

The present study adopted a qualitative methodology for performing analysis on empirical data conducted by IDC. Independent research with qualitative methodology to measure the performance benchmarks of SAP HANA in various industries was also conducted. Research was performed and documented with findings from various industries for reduction of complexity in the landscapes and introducing ground breaking innovation techniques to push the limits of ROI benefits. The ROI in academics for the University of Kentucky has shown 509% ROI in 5 years with the implementation of SAP HANA.

Red Bull has shown an ROI of 70%. CIR Food, Maple Leaf Foods, Molson Coors, Frucor have shown a reduction in the database with SAP HANA with compression technology from 80% to 511%. SAP HANA has reduced the usage of third-line of antibiotics from 5.8% to 1.2% at Seoul National University Hospital. Charité Universitätsmedizin Berlin implemented SAP HANA for Oncolyzer and analyzed data of 20 TB in few seconds. This contributed to the reduction of clinical trial period of 6 years of development. Mitsui Knowledge Industry implemented SAP HANA. MKI was able to perform genome-sequencing analysis on 3.2 billion pairs of DNA in 20 minutes.

Conclusions

This paper is a result of research about how SAP HANA, the in-memory computing database platform, has promoted the adoption of big data enterprise- ready solutions for enterprise applications and compared the results with its rival products such as Oracle Exadata, IBM DB2 BLU acceleration in the market. ROI benefits and performance benchmarks played a crucial role in bringing the awareness, adoption, interest, trial, and evolution of SAP HANA product in the market. SAP HANA has created a new wave of in-memory database computing at universities by resolving performance challenges for the academics spectrum, and contributed towards the improvement of graduation rates. IDC study has shown a savings of $6.17 million savings over a period of five years at the University of Kentucky. This is 509% ROI on SAP HANA implementation projected from the capital cost. The savings at the University of Kentucky has shown $210 thousand per year over a period of five years.

The data loads at the University of Kentucky have shown an improvement of 15 times from their previous RDBMS database tool data load operations. The data compression ratio has shown an improvement of 77% over traditional RDBMS database. The time to move the data from OLTP to OLAP was reduced by 87%. The reports from SAP HANA show an improvement of 80% in time-savings. Red Bull was a food and beverages industrial giant that has joined the apostle of the movement in 2011 to power their SAP NetWeaver BW by SAP HANA. The database with SAP HANA upgrade was reduced to 0.3GB from 1.5TB. CIR Food has implemented SAP HANA. CIR Food was able to analyze the reports in seconds as opposed to 20 minutes before SAP HANA implementation. CIR Food has measured a 70% improvement in the ROI after implementation.

Maple Leaf Foods SAP HANA implementation resulted in 25 reports by consolidating 500 business analytic reports. The reports showed the results in under a second with SAP HANA implementation for Maple Leaf Foods. Molson Coors had complex SAP landscape environment with multiple SAP BW instances and SAP ERP instances for each business unit. Due to this complexity, Molson Coors had to build prototypes for each environment that consumed approximately two weeks for each prototype. After SAP HANA implementation, the prototyping took only 1 day. ODS activations have shown a time savings of 70% to 80% for various scenarios. Frucor, a food, and beverages company, has shown a compression of 511% after SAP HANA implementation. SAP NetWeaver BW queries executed 10 times to100 times faster than the traditional RDBMS database.

The healthcare industry was revolutionized with groundbreaking speed in providing the analytics that could potentially save time and reduce clinical trial development. Seoul National University Hospital used to provide the third-line of antibiotics for five to six days prior to pre-surgery. The continued usage of third-line antibiotics can break the immunization system. SAP HANA analytics has reduced the usage of third-line antibiotics from 5.8% to 1.2% and subsequently to no third-line of antibiotics. Analyzing the condition of the blood cells and identifying the requirements, Seoul National University Hospital was able to determine the need of antibiotics for patients. Before implementing SAP HANA, Seoul National University Hospital was able to retrieve the data from 30 minutes to one hour for a data range of six months. However, SAP HANA analytics was able to retrieve the data for 10 years under two to three seconds.

Charité Universitätsmedizin Berlin was able to retrieve the data from reports with SAP HANA implementation for Oncolyzer under seconds on a 20TB database. Mitsui Knowledge Industry, a bioinformatics company researching genome sequencing, performed analysis on 3.2 billion DNA base pairs of the human genome in 20 minutes. Integration of SAP HANA with R language has shown an improvement of 400,000 times the speed for Mitsui Knowledge Industry. Medtronic, a medical devices company, has implemented SAP HANA. Before SAP HANA implementation, Medtronic experienced an execution time of BOBJ reports in three hours. After SAP HANA implementation, BOBJ reports ran in three minutes. Boston Scientific has seen an improvement of 3,600 times on BW report execution times after SAP HANA implementation.

TechAmerica Foundation has shown that $380b budget can be saved by big data tools. The city of Boston has implemented SAP HANA. After SAP HANA implementation, the inquiry calls for problematic properties was reduced by 66%. The number of license permits was reduced to 10 from 600. SAP HANA has provided 18 new score cards for the city's performance in 18 departments, boosted 911-call proactive monitoring, and reduced the crime rate by 55%.

The aerospace industry requires blazing performance of analytics. The aerospace industry has complex assembly manufacturing solutions that require several components to assemble the final product. This puts the aerospace industry in a unique position to process large chunks of data. Honeywell Aerospace has implemented the SAP HANA solution powering their BOBJ suite. Earlier BOBJ 3.0 with Oracle RDBMS database took around 12 hours to extract the data of 5TB. BOBJ 4.0 powered by SAP HANA was able to extract this data in one minute. Sagem, an SAFRAN Aerospace company, had RDBMS database size of 2.15 TB. The query execution after SAP HANA implementation has improved by 97% for Sagem. The database compression ratio has improved by 206%. SAP HANA database shrunk to 443GB from 2.15TB.

Several big data tools in the market were discussed in the present study and it was concluded that SAP HANA is the only enterprise-ready and big data ready solution with a single instance and columnar storage with native enterprise application integration that can be hosted with options of on premise, co-location, and cloud computing environments. SAP HANA has proved to be the fastest growing database and technology SAP has ever released, in the entire history of SAP, that can resolve performance challenges and reduce complexity of the landscape.

Discussion

In 2010, the Tokyo Institute of Technology invented data storage by encoding the data with lasers throughout the liquid crystals for permanent storage. CDs and DVDs can store the data on the surface; however, these only last up to few decades. In 2012, Hitachi heralded that they have stored the data permanently on a quartz glass plate that can withstand a temperature of 1,832 F. It is also waterproof. Andra, a French nuclear waste management agency is in the process of creating data on sapphire, and platinum discs that can last up to 10 million years.

In 2013, researchers at the University of Southampton in the UK have begun storing the data memory on five-dimensional silica glass discs with a laser. They have demonstrated that each disc can hold 360 TB of memory. This data can stay forever and does not get destroyed, unlike CDs and DVDs. The researchers at the University of Southampton call this data that "survives the human race" as it is estimated to last up to 10 billion years. The transactions in business occur metaphorically at the speed of light, and businesses require an agile systems that can process these transactions to stay competitive in the industry. The invention of permanent storage can resolve a great deal of conundrums in the industry to store data, but do not resolve the problems associated with speed of the retrieval of the data.

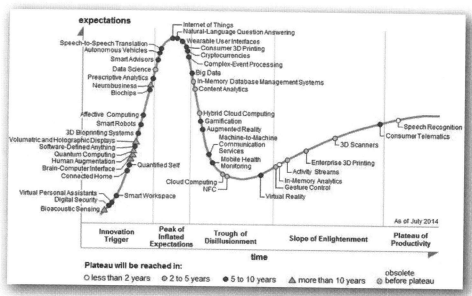

Figure 2. Gartner Hype Cycle for emerging technologies.

In today's world, organizations are unable to mine the data to perform real-time analytics, process the information, and harness the power of hardware with economies of scale. Aerospike jumped into the fray of in-memory computing with hybrid memory (DRAM and flash) providing depth of data analytics to spot trends in the business (Gartner, 2014). For a corporation, Aerospike reduced the footprint of servers from 184 to 10. The cost reduced from $2.5 million to $236,000 thousand. In October 2013, Aerospike was the only visionary in Gartner Magic quadrant. Over a long arc of time, business needs a nimble database with ACID properties. Gartner has recognized Aerospike, the world's fastest database, as one of the visionaries for 2014. DataStax, the company that delivers Apache Cassandra (a default choice for big data driven by organizations such as Barracuda Networks, Comcast, Constant Contact, eBay, and Netflix) to enterprises, has been recognized as the top visionary by Gartner for 2014.

In the Gartner Magic Quadrant for October 2014, SAP HANA is one of the leaders for operational database management systems (ODBMS). However, SAP HANA did not secure a position with the visionaries. This provides insights to SAP HANA to revolutionize the infrastructure model to run the database with alternative in-memory options. The Gartner hype cycle for emerging technologies 2014 has shown that big data, in-memory databases such as SAP HANA are two to five years from plateauing.

Recommendations

SAP HANA was built from the ground up to run entirely on DRAM. The cost of DRAM chips is reducing every year; however, flash memory is highly cost-effective as opposed to DRAM. The future outlook of in-memory databases appears to tilt towards flash memory. In a recent study, results showed that the cost of data in flash for 2 TB of database is $73, as opposed to data in-memory cost $1,209.

The cost-benefit ratio is 1:17. Aerospike is already running data in flash successfully, with high performance. DRAM in-memory database comes with limitations of scalability unlike in-memory data grids that can perform massively parallel processing on extensive and large sets of clusters of commodity servers. In the same example of the research, in-memory database (DRAM) required 50 nodes 2 TB database requirements; however, data in flash only required four nodes. The present study contains a strong recommendation to SAP HANA research labs to architect future SAP HANA database as data in flash to support tiered database storage and come up with revolutionary and innovative architecture in future models.

Currently, many customers globally are performing abstruse assessments to embrace SAP HANA into their organization. The cost is one of the main concerns. SAP HANA is now slightly above IBM DB2 as shown in Gartner Magic Quadrant for October 2014. However, it could not secure a position in visionaries. SAP should look at the options of economies of flash, and create a hybrid memory with the combination of flash and DRAM to capture a huge market segment.

SAP HANA for small companies can cost around $300,000 with software and hardware. Aerospike offers the database at 1 TB at $75,000 per year. The cost is a huge factor; SAP HANA requires a forklift upgrade similar to the database Aerospike to increase the number of domestic and global customers.

Speech-to-speech translation is now on the peak of emerging technologies for 2015. Microsoft's Research Labs has been working on natural language processing in collaboration with Bing on machine learning algorithms for speech. Microsoft aims to power

Skype with speech-to-speech translation next year, which will allow translating languages around the globe for the people who do not converse in the same language. Microsoft heretofore has won the battle of nerves with Apple, Google, and SAP in this area in terms of constructing the algorithms for machine learning with symmetrical architecture that powers Microsoft's Cortana. Partnering with Interactive Intelligence Customer Interaction Center, the 4.0 version has boosted SAP's ability to integrate and deploy IVR seamlessly on SAP CRM 7.X.

SAP HANA database has proven to work well with IVR system. IVR is already modern computer telephony integration for SAP CRM banking, service, and utility industries. IVR allows routing the calls to the appropriate recipients of the call on SAP CRM CIC (Customer Interaction Center). Earlier partnership of SAP with Microsoft to run SAP Business Suite, NetWeaver technology stack of solutions on Azure cloud has provided elasticity, scalability, and flexibility for enterprise performance. SAP HANA is progressively moving in the trough of disillusionment of emerging growth technologies. Organic development of speech-to-speech translation for SAP CRM powered by SAP HANA or integration with Microsoft's speech-to-speech translation can be a benefactor for global enterprises running SAP CRM. Though speech-to-speech translation technology trends are in rudimentary stages of development, these concepts are already underway, but in the next five to10 years, the technology trends can enable SAP HANA with speech-to-speech translation and voice recognition.

World's fastest supercomputer, Tianhe–2, has a blazing ultra-fast processor with peak performance of 33.86 petaflops measured on the Linpack benchmark. The human brain weighs about 3 pounds. According to research conducted by Azevedo et al.,[18] the human brain contains about 86 billion neurons. This research was an apostle of the movement in neuroscience. A single neuron in the brain can run at a maximum speed of 100 Hz. Inside the human brain, dendrites act as inputs that send the messages from one neuron to another neuron. Axons act as output zones at the other end that connect to thousands of neurons at the same time through electromagnetic signals. Neurotransmitters are chemicals that transmit the electrical signals from one neuron to another. Synaptic knobs link the pathways between axons. The transmission of a thought is ubiquitous. The thought does not have a location on a single neuron.

The biological evolution of brain's consciousness has taken thousands of years to revolutionize parallel processing. In brain, typically 86 billion neurons are parallel processing the data with massive clustering computation capabilities. Early computers processed the data on a single chip with the aid of an operating system and programs. R language with SAP HANA integration applies neural network learning algorithms to provide predictive analytics for enterprises in forecasting. R language computes with input and output nodes similar to the way neurons operate. Complex-event processing and ICT are emerging technologies that require a forklift upgrade to process the information. SAP HANA in future can build a natural language in ABAP based on neural networks to provide predictive analytics for future forecasting.

BIBLIOGRAPHY

Abadi, D., Boncz, P., & Harizopoulos, S. (2009). Column-oriented database systems. Retrieved November 1, 2015, from http://nms.csail.mit.edu/~stavros/pubs/tutorial2009-column_stores.pdf

Aerospike. (2014). Products and pricing. Retrieved November 3, 2014, from http://www.aerospike.com/products-services/

Amazon. (2011). Amazon elastic MapReduce: Developer guide. Retrieved December 31, 2013, from http://www.technicalwritingprofessional.com/images/emr-dg.pdf

Analytics, R. (2015). Optimizing Open Source R for Multi-Threaded Performance. Retrieved October 31, 2015, from http://www.revolutionanalytics.com/high-performance-r

Anderson, J. C., Lehnardt, J., & Slater, N. (2010). *CouchDB: The definitive guide* (1st ed.). Sebastopol, CA: O'Reilly Media.

Appleby, J. (2013). The top 10 SAP HANA myths spread by other vendors. Retrieved January 7, 2013, from http://www.saphana.com/community/blogs/blog/2013/07/18/the-top-10-sap-hana-myths-spread-by-other-vendors

Appleby, J. (2013). What in-memory database for SAP BW? A comparison of the major vendors. Retrieved January 8, 2014, from http://www.saphana.com/community/blogs/blog/2013/11/13/comparing-sap-hana-to-ibm-db2-blu-and-oracle-12-in-memory-for-sap-bw

Arxiv, T. (2013). The big data conundrum: How to define it? Retrieved November 9, 2013, from http://www.technologyreview.com/view/519851/the-big-data-conundrum-how-to-define-it/

Athow, D. (2013). How Talend is taking the pain out of big data. Retrieved December 20, 2013, from http://www.techradar.com/news/internet/data-centre/how-talend-plans-to-take-the-pain-out-of-big-data-1208837?src=rss&attr=all

Azevedo, F. A., Carvalho, L. R., Grinberg, L. T., Farfel, J. M., Leite, R. E., Jacob, W. F., & Herculano-Houzel, S. (2009). Equal numbers of neuronal and nonneuronal cells make the human brain an isometrically scaled-up primate brain. Retrieved December 7, 2014, from http://www.ncbi.nlm.nih.gov/pubmed/19226510

Baer, T. (2014). How SAP is refining its big data strategy. Retrieved January 7, 2013, from http://www.cloudcomputing-news.net/blog-hub/2014/jan/03/sap-refines-big-data-strategy/

Baragoin, C., Bercianos, J., Komel, J., Robinson, G., Sawa, R., & Schuinder, E. (2001). OLAP theory and practices . Retrieved May 13, 2014, from http://www.redbooks.ibm.com/redbooks/pdfs/sg246138.pdf

Berlin, C. U. (2011). Groundbreaking Intelligence for World-class Patient care . Retrieved July 29, 2014, from http://www.intel.com/content/dam/www/public/us/en/documents/case-studies/health-care-xeon-sap-charite-universitatsmedizin-berlin-study.pdf

Bertram, D., & Mathiowetz, R. (2014). Personalized Medicine Breaking New Ground in the Fight Against Cancer. Retrieved

August 4, 2014, from http://www.sap-innovationcenter.com/files/2014/02/DeepDive-Health.pdf

Bloom, A. (2013). McKinsey on Big Data Analytics: The #1 Key to US Economic Growth? Retrieved January 30, 2014, from https://blog.pivotal.io/pivotal/p-o-v/mckinsey-on-big-data-analytics-the-1-key-to-us-economic-growth

Bloomberg. (2014). Maple Leaf Foods Inc (MFI:Toronto). (2014, September 12). *Consumer staples sector.* Retrieved from http://investing.businessweek.com/research/stocks/earnings/earnings.asp?ticker=MFI:CN

Blum, B. (2013). Meet the 'Google Analytics of Beer.' Retrieved September 20, 2014, from http://www.israel21c.org/technology/meet-the-google-analytics-of-beer/

Bontempo, C., & Zagelow, G. (1998, September 1). The IBM data warehouse architecture. *Communications of the ACM, 41*(9), 38-48. http://dx.doi.org/10.1145/285070.285078

Borchert, A. (2012). SAP HANA – What's new: product update, use cases, case studies. Retrieved February 23, 2014, from http://global.sap.com/slovenia/about/events/2012/sap-innovation-day/pdf/2012_09_SL_InnovationDay_002.pdf

Boulton, C. (2012). Medtronic, the Medical Device Maker, Undergoes a Data Transplant. Retrieved August 5, 2014, from http://blogs.wsj.com/cio/2012/04/24/medtronic-the-medical-device-maker-undergoes-a-data-transplant/

Bracht, O. (2013). Five ways to handle Big Data in R. Retrieved October 31, 2015, from http://www.r-bloggers.com/five-ways-to-handle-big-data-in-r/

Cartwright, J. (2014). Wonder stuff: Glass that will store your info forever. Retrieved October 28, 2014, from http://www.newscientist.com/article/mg22429900.600-wonder-stuff-glass-that-will-store-your-info-for-ever.html

Cha, S. K. (2014). Prof. Sang Kyun Cha. Retrieved July 27, 2014, from http://kdb.snu.ac.kr/chask/

Channe, R. (2012). BW on HANA Basics and Differences. Retrieved November 27, 2013, from http://scn.sap.com/thread/3185998

Chainani, N., Lu, W., Burkleaux, A., & Nicola, M. (2013). DB2 with BLU acceleration: A rapid adoption guide. Retrieved January 7, 2014, from http://www.ibm.com/developerworks/data/library/techarticle/dm-1309db2bluaccel/dm-1309db2bluaccel-pdf.pdf

Charité. (2014). Charité - Berlin. Retrieved July 28, 2014, from http://www.molecular-medicine-berlin.com/en/about_us/charite/

Clabby Analytics. (2013). IBM DB2 BLU acceleration vs. SAP HANA vs. Oracle Exadata. Retrieved January 7, 2013, from http://www.clabbyanalytics.com/uploads/BLU.pdf

Codd, E. F. (1970). A relational model of data for large shared data banks. Retrieved January 12, 2015, from http://www.seas.upenn.edu/~zives/03f/cis550/codd.pdf

Coffman, K. G., & Odlyzko, A. (1998, October 5). The size and growth rate of the internet. First Monday, 3. Retrieved January 12, 2015, from http://firstmonday.org/ojs/index.php/fm/article/view/620/541

Conn, S. S. (2004). OLTP and OLAP data integration: A review of feasible implementation methods and architectures for real time data analysis. Retrieved April 25, 2014, from http://academic.regis.edu/cias/Library/pid54211.pdf

Couchbase. (2012). Why NoSQL? Three trends disrupting the database status quo. Retrieved November 9, 2013, from http://www.couchbase.com/why-nosql/nosql-database

Creswell, J. W. (2012). Educational research: Planning, conducting, and evaluating quantitative and qualitative research (4th ed.). Boston, MA: Pearson Education, Inc

Cronin, C. (2012). BW table types (MD tbl, SID tbl, DIM tbl, etc). Retrieved May 26, 2013, from http://wiki.sdn.sap.com/wiki/display/BI/BW+Table+Types+(MD+tbl,+SID+tbl,+DIM+tbl,+etc)

Datacamp (2014). What is the best statistical programming language? Infograph. Retrieved October 31, 2015, from http://blog.datacamp.com/statistical-language-wars-the-infograph/

Dave, P. (2013). big data - What is big data - 3 Vs of big data - volume, velocity and variety. Retrieved November 9, 2013, from http://blog.sqlauthority.com/2013/10/02/big-data-what-is-big-data-3-vs-of-big-data-volume-velocity-and-variety-day-2-of-21/

Dotson, K. (2014). Big Data needs drive R as a powerful enterprise ready language. Retrieved August 3, 2014, from http://siliconangle.com/blog/2014/07/28/big-data-needs-drive-r-as-a-powerful-enterprise-ready-language/

Downey, J. (2012). Exploring NoSQL: Redis. Retrieved 2012, from http://jimdowney.net/2012/02/07/exploring-nosql-redis/

Dragland, A. (2013). Big Data, for Better or Worse: 90% of World's Data Generated Over Last Two Years. Retrieved December 18, 2013, from http://www.sciencedaily.com/releases/2013/05/130522085217.htm

Eacrett, M. (2014). What is new in SAP HANA SPS 09. Retrieved January 23, 2015, from https://blogs.saphana.com/2014/10/21/what-is-new-in-sap-hana-sps-09/

Edjlali, R., & Schlegel, K. (2012). What does HANA mean for SAP BW customers? Retrieved November 9, 2013, from http://h10131.www1.hp.com/campaigns/hp-service-solution-saphana/what-does-hana-mean-224138.pdf

Einstein, D. (2013). How the Cloud and Big Data are changing entertainment . Retrieved December 24, 2013, from http://www.forbes.com/sites/netapp/2013/01/02/cloud-big-data-entertainment/

Eldrige, M. (n.d.). Understanding Tableau's Fast Data Engine. Retrieved November 1, 2015, from http://www.tableau.com/sites/default/files/pages/tcc11-fastdataengine.pdf

FAL Labs. (2011). Tokyo Cabinet: A modern implementation of DBM. Retrieved November 9, 2013, from http://fallabs.com/tokyocabinet/

FDA (2011). Understanding barriers to medical device quality. Retrieved August 5, 2014, from http://www.fda.gov/downloads/AboutFDA/CentersOffices/CDRH/CDRHReports/UCM277323.pdf

Feinberg, D., Adrian, M., & Heudecker, N. (2014). NoSQL databases, Hadoop, big data : Pinned tabs Oct.31th. Retrieved November 3, 2014, from http://nosql.mypopescu.com/post/101404751771/nosql-databases-hadoop-big-data-pinned-tabs-oct-31th

FlashDBA (2012). In Memory Databases: HANA, Exadata X3 and Flash Memory (Part 2). Retrieved January 20, 2015, from http://flashdba.com/2012/10/10/in-memory-databases-part2/

Florenzano, E. (2009). No SQL - Tokyo Cabinet / Tokyo Tyrant. Retrieved November 9, 2013, from http://eflorenzano.com/blog/2009/07/21/my-thoughts-nosql/

Floyer, D. (2012). Data in DRAM is a flash in the pan. Retrieved September 12, 2014, from http://wikibon.org/wiki/v/Data_in_DRAM_is_a_Flash_in_the_Pan

Frucor (2014). Frucor - Our Company. Retrieved September 16, 2014, from http://www.frucor.co.nz/index.php/our_company/

Gahm, H. (2013). HANA column store backgrounds (INSERT ONLY). Retrieved January 10, 2014, from http://scn.sap.com/community/

abap/hana/blog/2013/08/15/hana-column-store-backgrounds-insert-only

Gantz, J. F., Reinsel, D., Chute, C., Schlichting, W., McArthur, J., Minton, S., ... Manfrediz, A. (2007). The expanding digital universe: A forecast of worldwide information growth through 2010. Retrieved January 12, 2015, from http://www.emc.com/collateral/analyst-reports/expanding-digital-idc-white-paper.pdf

GAO, U. (1990). Qualitative data analysis: Program evaluation and methodology division, GAO, case study evaluations. Retrieved February 10, 2013, from http://www.gao.gov/special.pubs/10_1_9.pdf

Gartner (2012). Gartner identifies fast-moving technologies with hype cycle report. Retrieved January 12, 2015, from http://electroiq.com/blog/2012/08/gartner-identifies-fast-moving-technologies-with-hype-cycle-report/

Gartner (2014). Aerospike recognized as a visionary in Gartner 2014 Magic Quadrant for Operational Database Management Systems. Retrieved November 3, 2014, from http://www.aerospike.com/press-releases/aerospike-visionary-in-gartner-2014-mq-odbms/

Gartner (2014). Gartner's 2014 hype cycle for emerging technologies maps the journey to digital business. Retrieved November 23, 2014, from http://www.gartner.com/newsroom/id/2819918

Genome Gov (2010). The Human Genome Project Completion: Frequently Asked Questions. Retrieved August 4, 2014, from http://www.genome.gov/11006943

Gallagher, J. (2014). DNA project 'to make UK world genetic research leader'. Retrieved August 3, 2014, from http://www.bbc.com/news/health-28488313

Glover, A. (2012). Flexing NoSQL: MongoDB in review. Retrieved November 9, 2013, from http://www.javaworld.com/javaworld/jw-02-2012/120208-mongodb-review.html?page=1

Goebel, N. (2013). A quick introduction to Apache Cassandra. Retrieved November 9, 2013, from http://www.sitepoint.com/a-quick-introduction-to-apache-cassandra/

Goodell, M. (2014). Big data sessions at ASUG User Conference and SAPPHIRENow. Retrieved August 28, 2014, from http://www.saphana.com/community/blogs/blog/2014/05/27/big-data-sessions-at-asug-user-conference-and-sapphirenow

Grob, M. (2013). SID Tables in #SAP #BW. Retrieved January 26, 2014, from http://scn.sap.com/docs/DOC-48736

GSK (2013). Tomorrow's World - Creating the future together. Retrieved August 1, 2014, from http://www.assima.net/images/resources/customer-events/UKISUG13_Presentation_GSK.pdf

Gunawan, F. (2014). Build an interactive voice response (IVR) system connected to SAP HANA - Part 1. Retrieved November 23, 2014, from http://scn.sap.com/community/developer-center/hana/blog/2014/07/16/build-an-interactive-voice-response-ivr-system-connected-to-sap-hana--part-1

Hamilton, A. (2013). IBM snaps up Aspera to accelerate big data. Retrieved December 21, 2013, from http://www.techradar.com/us/news/internet/cloud-services/ibm-snaps-up-aspera-to-accelerate-big-data-1210083?src=rss&attr=all

Hare, K. W. (2012). A comparison of SQL and NoSQL databases. Retrieved November 9, 2013, from http://www.slideshare.net/Muratakal/rdbms-vs-nosql-15797058

Harris, A. (2013). A Quick Guide to IBM's Analytics Acquisitions, Strategy. Retrieved October 26, 2013, from http://siliconangle.com/blog/2013/02/05/a-quick-guide-to-ibms-analytics-acquisitions-strategy/

Harris, D. (2013). IBM acquires Aspera and its tech for moving massive files to the cloud. Retrieved December 23, 2013, from https://gigaom.com/2013/12/19/ibm-acquires-aspera-and-its-tech-for-moving-massive-files-to-the-cloud/

Hazan, E. (2013). Digital revolution: Six trends for the media industry. Retrieved December 24, 2013, from http://www.slideshare.net/McK_CMSOForum/turning-the-digital-revolution-into-an-opportunity-for-the-media-industry

Hazan, E., & Banfi, F. (2013). http://www.mckinsey.com/client_service/marketing_and_sales/latest_thinking/leveraging_big_data_to_optimize_digital_marketing. Retrieved December 26, 2014, from http://www.mckinsey.com/client_service/marketing_and_sales/latest_thinking/leveraging_big_data_to_optimize_digital_marketing

Hazan, E., Meffert, J., Wagener, N., Chappuis, B., & Duncan, E. (2013). Telecommunications, Media, and Technology. Retrieved December 25, 2014, from https://www.google.com/url?sa=t& rct=j&q=&esrc=s&source=web&cd=2&cad=rja&uact=8&ved= 0CCMQFjABahUKEwjaj8Gkl4nJAhVCpIgKHWpyB54&u rl=https%3A%2F%2Fwww.mckinsey.com%2F~%2Fmedia% 2Fmckinsey%2Fdotcom%2Fclient_service%2FHigh%2520T ech%2FPDFs%2FTMT_iConsumers_Life_online_2013-01. ashx&usg=AFQjCNE1-RTrO0SS0cVRRy6lewJyF1l6ew&sig 2=fxOdE0Et7qSURP5IDBW2ZA&bvm=bv.106923889,d.cGU

Heimer, A. (2011). SAP HANA: Understanding in-memory computing. Retrieved January 12, 2015, from http://www.sapsa.se/wp-content/uploads/2011/12/9-SAP-HANA-V%C3%A5rImpuls-2012.pdf

Henschen, D. (2011). 12 brawny business intelligence products for SMBs. Retrieved May 26, 2013, from http://www.information-week.com/smb/hardware-software/12-brawny-business-intelligence-products/230600071

Henschen, D. (2013). IBM And Big Data Disruption: Insider's View. Retrieved January 18, 2014, from http://www.informationweek.com/big-data/big-data-analytics/ibm-and-big-data-disruption-insiders-view/d/d-id/1110680?page_number=2

Howson, C. (2013). 7 top business intelligence trends for 2013. Retrieved May 26, 2013, from http://www.informationweek.com/software/business-intelligence/7-top-business-intelligence-trends-for-2/240146994

HP (2013). Turn information into advantage Disaster Tolerant HP AppSystems for SAP HANA. Retrieved January 25, 2014, from http://h20195.www2.hp.com/V2/GetPDF.aspx%2F4AA4-6031ENW.pdf

IBM (2010). IBM Completes Acquisition Of Netezza. Retrieved October 15, 2014, from https://www-03.ibm.com/press/us/en/pressrelease/32955.wss

IBM (2012). Smarter Analytics for Government. Retrieved December 23, 2013, from https://www-950.ibm.com/events/wwe/grp/grp004.nsf/vLookupPDFs/Rehan%20Sadiq's%20Presentation/$file/Rehan%20Sadiq's%20Presentation.pdf

IBM (2013). IBM DB2 enhances performance for SAP solutions. Retrieved December 21, 2013, from http://www.ibm.com/solutions/sap/us/en/landing/J233701A22235G06/db2sap.html

IBM (2013). SAP support for IBM DB2 with BLU acceleration. Retrieved January 7, 2014, from http://ibmdatamag.com/2013/12/sap-support-for-ibm-db2-with-blu-acceleration/

IBM (2013). Pure Data System. Retrieved December 21, 2013, from http://www.ibm.com/ibm/puresystems/us/en/pf_puredata.html

IBM (2013). The Cost/Benefit Case for IBM PureData System for Analytics. Retrieved December 21, 2013, from http://ibmdatamag.com/2013/05/itg-analyst-paper-costbenefit-case-for-ibm-pure-data-system-for-analytics-comparing-costs-and-time-to-value-with-teradata-data-warehouse-appliance-itg/

IBM (n.d.). http://www.ibm.com/ibm/puresystems/us/en/puredata-system-for-analytics.html. Retrieved January 7, 2014, from http://www.ibm.com/ibm/puresystems/us/en/puredata-system-for-analytics.html

IDC (2013). The challenge of information delay. Retrieved May 15, 2014, from http://www.gettingdowntorealtimebusiness.com/challenge-of-information-delay.html

IDC (2014). About IDC. Retrieved April 13, 2014, from http://www.idc.com/about/about.jsp

IISTechnology (2013). Big data solutions for hospitals and health care. Retrieved February 5, 2014, from http://www.iisl.com/user-files/files/eGuide-Layout-BD_Hospitals_and_Health_Care.pdf

Intel (2013). SAP* HANA and Intel® distribution of Apache Hadoop* for SAP software engineered for real-time big data analytics. Retrieved January 1, 2014, from http://hadoop.intel.com/pdfs/IDH_SAP_HANA_Product_Brief.pdf

Interactive Intelligence Group (2014). Interactive Intelligence Customer Interaction Center® (CIC) Software Achieves Certified Integration with SAP® CRM. Retrieved January 30, 2015, from http://investors.inin.com/releasedetail.cfm?releaseid=821589

Intuit (2015). A timeline of database history. Retrieved January 12, 2015, from http://quickbase.intuit.com/articles/timeline-of-database-history

Jones, K. (1998). An introduction to data warehousing: What are the implications for the Network? *International Journal of Network Management*, 8, 42-56.

Kanaracus, C. (2012). Three Analyst Predictions for 2013: Hadoop, SAP, and MySQL vs NoSQL. Retrieved November 27, 2013, from http://nosql.mypopescu.com/post/38214093612/three-analyst-predictions-for-2013-hadoop-sap-and

Kaufhold, G. (2010). The digital entertainment revolution. Retrieved February 23, 2013, from http://www.capgemini.com/m/en/tl/The_Digital_Entertainment_Revolution_.pdf

Kelly, J. (2013). Primer on SAP HANA. Retrieved November 3, 2014, from http://wikibon.org/wiki/v/Primer_on_SAP_HANA

Kelly, S. M. (2012). Google Fiber TV Coming Soon to a Living Room Near You. Retrieved February 23, 2013, from http://mashable.com/2012/07/26/google-fiber-tv/#4Bu1RAfr1mqp

Klopp, R. (2013). IBM BLU and SAP HANA. Retrieved January 7, 2014, from http://robklopp.wordpress.com/2013/08/20/ibm-blu-and-sap-hana/

Klopp, R. (2013). OLTP + BI in a single HANA instance. Retrieved May 13, 2014, from http://www.saphana.com/community/blogs/blog/2013/01/03/oltp-bi-in-a-single-hana-instance

Klopp, R. (2013). Some unaudited HANA performance numbers. Retrieved May 13, 2014, from http://robklopp.wordpress.com/2013/03/29/some-unaudited-hana-performance-numbers/

Kovshenin, K. (n.d.). Tag archives: Neural network. Retrieved December 8, 2014, from https://beckmw.wordpress.com/tag/neural-network/

Krouse, J. (2014). Millenials benefit from big data at the University of Kentucky. Retrieved May 15, 2014, from http://scn.sap.com/community/higher-education-and-research/blog/2014/04/21/millenials-benefit-from-big-data-at-the-university-of-kentucky

Lampitt, A. (2013). Big movies, big data: Netflix embraces NoSQL in the cloud. Retrieved December 31, 2013, from http://www.info-world.com/d/big-data/big-movies-big-data-netflix-embraces-nosql-in-the-cloud-217765?page=0,1

Laney, D. (2001). 3D data management: Controlling data volume, velocity, and variety. Retrieved January 12, 2015, from http://blogs.gartner.com/doug-laney/files/2012/01/ad949-3D-Data-Management-Controlling-Data-Volume-Velocity-and-Variety.pdf

Lawler, R. (2014). Microsoft demos real-time speech-to-speech translation on Skype. Retrieved November 23, 2014, from http://techcrunch.com/2014/05/27/microsoft-demoes-real-time-speech-to-speech-translation-on-skype/

Lintelman, L., & Brague, C. (2012). Got Dirty Data? We Have the Solution! . Retrieved December, 2014, from https://archivesap-techedhandson.hana.ondemand.com/contentArchive/EIM265.pdf

Lohr, S. (2013). The origins of 'big data': An etymological detective story. Retrieved January 12, 2015, from http://bits.blogs.nytimes.com/2013/02/01/the-origins-of-big-data-an-etymological-detective-story/

Loo, J., & Anjum, Z. (2014). The CIO Interview: Hee Hwang, CIO at SNU Bundang Hospital, South Korea. Retrieved July

27, 2014, from http://news.idg.no/cw/art.cfm?id=F2D96BFF-C2D7-6101-9813DA7A2D7958F4

Lucas, S. (2014). SAP HANA everywhere from startups to long-standing SAP customers worldwide are harnessing in-memory computing. Retrieved August 19, 2014, from http://sapinsider.wispubs.com/Assets/Articles/2014/July/SPI-SAP-HANA-everywhere?utm_source=WIS&utm_medium=Email&utm_campaign=HANA_Q3SR

Lyman, P., & Varian, H. R. (2000, December). How much information? The journal of electronic publishing, 6. http://dx.doi.org/http://dx.doi.org/10.3998/3336451.0006.204

Madler, M. (2013). Digital revolution prompts Warner Bros. management changes. Retrieved May 30, 2013, from http://www.sfvbj.com/news/2013/may/16/digital-revolution-prompts-warner-bros-management-/

Mashey, J. R. (1998). Big data ... and the next wave of InfraStress. Retrieved January 12, 2015, from http://static.usenix.org/event/usenix99/invited_talks/mashey.pdf

McGinnis, J. (2013). Talend Reinforces Leadership in Big Data Integration with Support for YARN. Retrieved December 20, 2013, from http://www.reuters.com/article/2013/10/29/ny-talend-idUSnBw295523a+100+BSW20131029

McLellan, C. (2014). Analysing the analysts: Predicting emerging technologies. Retrieved January 22, 2015, from http://www.zdnet.com/article/analysing-the-analysts-predicting-emerging-technologies/

MDDI (2013). Top 40 medical device companies . Retrieved August 5, 2014, from http://www.mddionline.com/article/top-40-medical-device-companies

Mishra, P. (2013). Inside India's Aadhar, The World's Biggest Biometrics Database. Retrieved December 8, 2013, from http://techcrunch.com/2013/12/06/inside-indias-aadhar-the-worlds-biggest-biometrics-database/

Miller, J. (2014). IRS' approach to big data focuses on business outcomes. Retrieved December 1, 2014, from http://federalnewsradio.com/management/2014/09/irs-approach-to-big-data-focuses-on-business-outcomes/

Mochiko, T. (2014). Security a risk for 'Internet of Things'. Retrieved July 30, 2014, from http://www.bizcommunity.com/Article/196/544/116725.html

MongoDB. (2013). MongoDB production deployments. Retrieved November 9, 2013, from http://www.mongodb.org/about/production-deployments/

Moore, W. E., & Sheldon, E. B. (1968). *Indicators of Social Change: Concepts and Measurements by Eleanor Bernert Sheldon, Wilbert E. Moore (1968) Hardcover.* New York, NY: Russell Sage Foundation.

Morrison, T. (2012). SAP announces additional support for Hadoop. Retrieved January 27, 2014, from http://searchsap.techtarget.com/news/2240169183/SAP-announces-additional-support-for-Hadoop

Mosic, R. (2013). Real-time, Hybrid OLTP/OLAP now possible with columnar, in-memory databases. Retrieved May 13, 2014 , from http://rankomosic.sys-con.com/node/2850110

Munro, D. (2013). SAS And GSK Pull Big Pharma Into Big Data Collaboration. Retrieved August 1, 2014, from http://www.forbes.com/sites/danmunro/2013/06/27/sas-and-gsk-pull-big-pharma-into-big-data-collaboration/

Murphy, S. (2012). Google Fiber TV coming soon to a living room near you. Retrieved February 23, 2013, from http://mashable.com/2012/07/26/google-fiber-tv/

Murphy, S. (2012). How Google Fiber stacks up against Verizon FiOS. Retrieved February 23, 2013, from http://mashable.com/2012/08/21/google-fiber-verizon-fios/

NASA (n.d.). Dynamic design: Launch and propulsion. Retrieved August 29, 2014, from http://genesismission.jpl.nasa.gov/educate/scimodule/LaunchPropulsion/LP_PDFs/C4_STdeltarocket.pdf

Namey, E., Guest, G., Thairu, L., & Johnson, L. (2007). Data reduction techniques for large qualitative data sets . Retrieved February 10, 2013 , from http://www.stanford.edu/~thairu/07_184.Guest.1sts.pdf

Neuman, W. L. (2003). *Social Research Methods: Qualitative and Quantitative Approaches* (5th ed.). Boston, MA: Pearson Education, Inc.

Neuman, W. L. (2011). *Basics of Social Research: Qualitative and Quantitative Approaches* (3rd ed.). Boston, MA: Pearson Education Inc.

Newswire (2014). U.S. Neuromodulation Market Trends and Outlook to 2020: Led by Medtronic, Boston Scientific and St. Jude Medical. Retrieved August 5, 2014, from http://www.marketwatch.com/story/us-neuromodulation-market-trends-and-outlook-to-2020-led-by-medtronic-boston-scientific-and-st-jude-medical-2014-08-05?reflink=MW_news_stmp

Nicolaou, A. (2014). The 9 Best languages for crunching data. Retrieved October 31, 2015, from http://www.fastcompany.com/3030716/the-9-best-languages-for-crunching-data

Normandeau, K. (2013). Beyond volume, variety and velocity is the issue of big data veracity. Retrieved November 9, 2013, from http://inside-bigdata.com/2013/09/12/beyond-volume-variety-velocity-issue-big-data-veracity/

Northcutt, S. (2012). Project Management for Security Managers: Develop a plan. Retrieved August 25, 2013, from http://www.sans.edu/research/management-laboratory/article/mgt512-develop-plan

Ohri, A. (2014). *R for Cloud Computing: An Approach for Data Scientists.* New York City, NY: Springer .

Olofson, C. W., & Morris, H. D. (2011). Faster, Higher, Stronger: In-Memory computing disruption and what SAP HANA means for your organization. Retrieved November 9, 2011, from https://www.sapvirtualagency.com/FileExplorer/Partners/SAP%20Business%20Analytics%20Solutions/Web%20Feed/HANA/Faster,_Higher,_Stronger__In-Memory_Computing_Disruption_and_What_SAP_HANA_Means_for_Your_Organization.pdf

Olofson, C. W. (2012). Big data: Trends, strategies, and SAP technology, the dawn of the intelligent economy. Retrieved November 9, 2013, from http://www.sap.com/bin/sapcom/downloadasset.idc-report--big-data-trends-strategies-and-sap-technology-pdf.html

Olofson, C. W., & Morris, H. D. (2013). Blending transactions and analytics in a single in-memory platform: Key to the real-time enterprise: Sponsored by SAP. Retrieved April 13th, 2014, from http://www.saphana.com/servlet/JiveServlet/previewBody/4132-102-2-8712/Blending%20Transactions%20and%20Analytics%20into%20a%20Single%20in-memory%20Platform%20IDC....pdf

Oracle (2013). Oracle Exadata Database Machine X4-2. Retrieved January 24, 2015, from http://www.oracle.com/technetwork/database/exadata/exadata-dbmachine-x4-2-ds-2076448.pdf

Ortner, R., & Pietzka, D. (2012). OLTP, OLAP, SAP, and data warehouse. Retrieved May 13, 2014, from http://institute.unileoben.ac.at/infotech/lehre/infolog/SS2012/unterlagen/unit8.pdf

Palmer, M. (2014). Frucor Beverages - Fujitsu Power Appliance for the SAP HANA® platform. Retrieved September 17, 2014, from http://www.fujitsu.com/global/Images/Fujitsu-Frucor-CaseStudy.pdf

Panczenko, J. (2012). Developing evaluation measures for the second stage next generation engine on evolved expendable launch vehicles. Retrieved August 29, 2014, from http://www.dtic.mil/dtic/tr/fulltext/u2/a561904.pdf

Park, S. (2011). The future memory technologies. Retrieved January 23, 2015, from http://www.sematech.org/meetings/archives/symposia/10202/Keynote-Intro/Park_The%20future%20memory%20technologies.pdf

Patel, H. (2013). HANA curious - smart data access. Retrieved January 7, 2013, from http://www.saphana.com/community/learn/startups/blog/2013/08/21/hana-curious--smart-data-access

Penn, Schoen & Berland Associates, LLC. (2013). Big data and the public sector: A survey of IT decision makers in Federal and State public sectors. Retrieved August 23, 2014, from http://www.techamericafoundation.org/content/wp-content/uploads/2013/02/SAP-Public-Sector-Big-Data-Report_FINAL-2.pdf

Pivotal. (2013). Who's using Redis? Retrieved November 9, 2013, from http://redis.io/topics/whos-using-redis

Plattner, H. (2009). A common database approach for OLTP and OLAP using an in-memory column database. Retrieved May 7, 2014, from http://www.sigmod09.org/images/sigmod1ktp-plattner.pdf

Poggio, F. (2013). Readers Write: Big Data – The Next HIT/EMR Boondoggle? Retrieved December 23, 2013, from http://histalk2.com/2013/09/09/readers-write-big-data-the-next-hitemr-boondoggle/

Preimesberger, C. (2013). Apple Gets Big Data Analytics, Buys Topsy Labs for $200M. Retrieved November 29, 2013, from http://www.eweek.com/apple/apple-gets-big-data-analytics-buys-topsy-labs-for-200m.html

Press, G. (2013). A Very Short History Of Big Data. Retrieved December 1, 2014, from http://www.forbes.com/sites/gilpress/2013/05/09/a-very-short-history-of-big-data/

Price, D. (1961). *Science Since Babylon.* New Haven, CT: Yale University Press.

Price, D. J. (1975). *Science since Babylon.* New Haven, CT: Yale University Press.

Purdue University. (2010). Threats to security. Retrieved August 25, 2013, from http://www.cerias.purdue.edu/assets/pdf/k-12/info-sec_newsletters/03threats.pdf

Qlik (2011). What's new in QlikView 11. Retrieved November 2, 2015, from https://community.qlik.com/thread/45871

Qlik (2015). Make stunning data discoveries . Retrieved November 2, 2015, from http://www.qlik.com/products/qlik-sense

Qlik (2015). Our history. Retrieved November 2, 2015, from http://www.qlik.com/company/about-the-company/history

Quirk (n.d.). *City of Boston uses SAP HANA to improve citizens' experience.* [Video file]. Retrieved from http://www.saphana.com/community/learn/customer-stories/

Raman, V., Attaluri, G., Barber, R., Chainani, N., Kalmuk, D., Kulandaisamy, V., ... Lightstone, S. (2013). DB2 with BLU acceleration: So much more than just a column store. Retrieved January

7, 2014, from http://researcher.watson.ibm.com/researcher/files/us-ipandis/vldb13db2blu.pdf

Real-Time Innovations Inc. (2014). http://www.slideshare.net/RealTimeInnovations/connected-medical-devices-in-the-internet-of-things. (2014). Retrieved July 30, 2014, from http://www.slideshare.net/RealTimeInnovations/connected-medical-devices-in-the-internet-of-things

Real-Time Innovations Inc. (2014). Minimally Invasive Robotic Surgery (MIRS) with the DLR MiroSurge. Retrieved July 30, 2014, from http://www.rti.com/docs/German_Aerospace_Center_DLR.pdf

Real Time Innovations Inc (2014). RTI Presents "Internet of Things (IoT) Costs, Connectivity, Resources and Software" Complimentary Webinar. Retrieved April 14, 2015, from https://www.rti.com/company/news/iot-connectivity-webinar.html

ReportsnReports (2013). Managed Services Market to Grow at CAGR of 12.4% to 2018 in a New Research Report Now Available at ReportsnReports.com. Retrieved January 21, 2014, from http://www.prweb.com/releases/managed-services-market/08/prweb11021581.htm

ReportLinker (2014). It Hosting Industry: Market Research Reports, Statistics and Analysis. Retrieved January 21, 2014, from http://www.reportlinker.com/ci02077/It-Hosting.htm

Richter, R. (2012). HANA Speeds Cancer Research and Results. Retrieved July 28, 2014, from http://scn.sap.com/community/

hana-in-memory/blog/2012/04/04/hana-speeds-cancer-research-and-results

Rider, F. (1944). *The Scholar and the Future of the Research Library. A Problem and Its Solution.* New York, NY: Hadham Press.

Rosario, R. R. (2010). Taking R to the Limit (High Performance Computing in R), Part 2 -- Large Datasets, LA R Users' Group 8/17/10. Retrieved October 31, 2015, from http://www.slideshare.net/bytemining/r-hpc

SAP (2008). System Copy for SAP systems based on SAPNetWeaver 7.0 SR3ABAP. Retrieved May 14, 2014, from http://www.sdn.sap.com/irj/scn/go/portal/prtroot/docs/library/uuid/00f3087e-2620-2b10-d58a-c50b66c1578e?QuickLink=index&overridelayout=true&29665339138211

SAP. (2011). Analytic Views - What they are and how are they used? Retrieved November 27, 2013, from http://www.saphana.com/docs/DOC-1256

SAP (2011). SAP HANA Overview and roadmap. Retrieved November 9, 2013, from http://www.sdn.sap.com/irj/scn/go/portal/prtroot/docs/library/uuid/b0bb760d-809d-2e10-2d8d-baef578f4aa6?overridelayout=true

SAP (2012). Honeywell Aerospace: Running business in real time. Retrieved August 27, 2014, from http://www.sap.com/australia/solution/industry/aerospace-defense/customer-reviews.html

SAP (2012). Innovation done your way with custom solutions powered by SAP HANA®. Retrieved April 14, 2014, from http://www.sap.com/bin/sapcom/en_us/downloadasset.2012-05-may-29-06.innovation-done-your-way-with-custom-solutions-powered-by-sap-hana-pdf.html

SAP (2012). The agile aerospace and defense enterprise. Retrieved August 27, 2014, from http://www.sap.com/bin/sapcom/en_us/downloadasset.2012-12-dec-27-07.industry-executive-overview-aerospace-and-defense-the-agile-aerospace-and-defense-enterprise-pdf.html

SAP (2013). BI information integration: Key areas. Retrieved May 26, 2013, from http://help.sap.com/saphelp_nw70/helpdata/en/0c/58497f411a7848985ae2aa0dda0bd3/content.htm

SAP (2013). CIO Guide: How to Use Hadoop with Your SAP® Software Landscape. Retrieved January 27, 2014, from http://www.sapbigdata.com/wp-content/uploads/2013/08/PATS_CIO-Guide_Hadoop-in-SAP-Landscape_final_May-22.pdf

SAP (2013). Companies to Deliver Innovative, High-Performance Solutions that Combine SAP HANA® Platform With Industry Applications from SAS. Retrieved August 5, 2014, from http://global.sap.com/press.epx?pressid=21767

SAP (2013). Data Acquisition. Retrieved December 18, 2013, from http://help.sap.com/saphelp_nw73EhP1/helpdata/en/4a/2711cecfcf1cc5e10000000a42189b/frameset.htm

SAP (2013). Empower BI users with Enterprise Self-Services and Visualization. Retrieved June 20, 2013, from http://www.sap.com/asset/index.epx?id=201b8dc6-a0cd-4f28-b297-5f9a6d962d6c&name=Empower-Users-with-Enterprise-Self-Services-and-Visualization&_=1369271856504

SAP (2013). In-Memory Computing (SAP HANA) Services. Retrieved November 26, 2013, from http://www.sap.com/services-support/svc/in-memory-computing/customer-reviews.html

SAP (2013). Meeting the challenges of business intelligence. Retrieved January 9, 2015, from http://www.sap.com/bin/sap-com/cs_cz/downloadasset.2013-09-sep-10-21.meeting-the-challenges-of-business-intelligence-for-small-enterprises-pdf.html

SAP (2013). Real-time Information with SAP HANA means faster patient treatment at Charité. Retrieved July 28, 2014, from http://www.joomag.com/magazine/sap-forum-2013/0874753001369220922?page=101

SAP (2013). SAP HANA Enterprise Cloud. Retrieved August 3, 2014, from http://www.sap.com/bin/sapcom/en_us/downloadasset.2013-05-may-06-20.sap-hana-enterprise-cloud-pdf.html

SAP (2013). SAP and Technical University Munich Decode Human Proteome and Make Data Available for Biomedical Research. Retrieved August 4, 2014, from http://global.sap.com/corporate-en/news.epx?PressID=21099

SAP (2013). Starting SAP HANA Studio & Administration Console. Retrieved November 26, 2013, from https://

cookbook.experiencesaphana.com/bw/operating-bw-on-hana/hana-database-administration/administration-tools/starting-hana-studio-admin-console/

SAP AG (2013). SAP HANA Studio -Overview. Retrieved November 26, 2013, from http://www.saphana.com/docs/DOC-1217

SAP (2013). What's Dirty Data Costing You? Retrieved December 12, 2013, from http://www.slideshare.net/SAPTechnology/whats-dirty-data-costing-you

SAP (2014). 1736976 - Sizing report for BW on HANA. Retrieved May 14, 2014, from https://websmp130.sap-ag.de/sap (bD1lbiZjPTAwMQ==)/bc/bsp/sno/ui_entry/entry.htm?param=69765F6D6F64653D3030312669765F7361706E6F7465735F6E75 6D6265723D3137333639373626

SAP (2014). Accelerated inbox search. Retrieved April 13th, 2014, from http://help.sap.com/saphelp_crm700_ehp01/helpdata/en/e7/1e512833ef4a70a2c4da589adc48c6/content.htm?frameset=/en/1d/d89395e971457b8b999c2566d5a1e1/frameset.htm

SAP (2014). Aerospace and Defense Co. Sagem enhances their IT performance with SAP HANA. Retrieved August 27, 2014, from http://www.saphana.com/docs/DOC-4626

SAP (2014). BW on SAP HANA. Retrieved May 14, 2014, from https://cookbook.experiencesaphana.com/bw/deploying-bw-on-hana/preparation/plan-and-purchase-hana-system/

SAP. (2014). Hospital of the Future for Patients of Today. Retrieved July 28, 2014, from http://www.sap.com/customer-testimonials/healthcare/charite.html

SAP (2014). Its own first customer . Retrieved January 20, 2015, from http://www.sapdatacenter.com/article/sap_runs_sap/

SAP (2014). Rapid database migration of SAP BW to SAP HANA. Retrieved May 14, 2014, from https://websmp104.sap-ag.de/~form/handler?_APP=00200682500000002672&_EVENT=DISPLAY&_SCENARIO=&_HIER_KEY=501100035870000019235&_HIER_KEY=601100035870000260755&_HIER_KEY=601100035870000260778&_HIER_KEY=601100035870000260859&_HIER_KEY=601100035870000261038&

SAP (2014). SAP CRM on SAP HANA. Retrieved April 14, 2014, from https://cookbook.experiencesaphana.com/crm/what-is-crm-on-hana/

SAP (2014). SAP HANA (in-memory Computing) - Rely on hardware from global technology leaders. Retrieved January 7, 2014, from http://www.sap.com/pc/tech/in-memory-computing-hana/partners.html

SAP (2014). SAP® Business Warehouse powered by SAP HANA®. Retrieved January 22, 2015, from http://www.sap.com/bin/sapcom/ro_ro/downloadasset.2014-09-sep-16-23.business-warehouse-on-sap-hana-pdf.html

SAP (2014). Screening for Cancer in Real-Time. Retrieved August 1, 2014, from http://www.sap.com/customer-testimonials/professional-services/mitsui.html

SAP (2014). State of Indiana chooses SAP HANA platform to help fight infant mortality. Retrieved August 27, 2014, from http://www.news-sap.com/state-indiana-chooses-sap-hana-platform-help-fight-infant-mortality/

SAP (2015). SAP announces preliminary fourth quarter and full year 2014 results. Retrieved January 20, 2015, from http://www.news-sap.com/sap-announces-preliminary-fourth-quarter-full-year-2014-results-2/

SAP (2015). SAP HANA Named a Leader Among In-Memory Database Platforms by Independent Research Firm. Retrieved November 1, 2015, from http://news.sap.com/sap-hana-named-leader-among-memory-database-platforms-independent-research-firm/

SAP (n.d.). *City of Boston uses SAP HANA to improve citizens' experience.* [Video file]. Retrieved from http://www.saphana.com/community/learn/customer-stories/

SAP (n.d.). Data Compression in the Column Store. Retrieved March 10, 2015, from http://help.sap.com/saphelp_hanaplatform/help-data/en/bd/9017c8bb571014ae79efaeb46940f3/content.htm

SAP (n.d.). Global Healthcare and "Big Data". Retrieved July 30, 2014, from http://www.saphana.com/servlet/JiveServlet/previewBody/3631-102-1-7506/Healthcare%20paper.pdf

SAPHANA (n.d.). Column Vs Row Data Storage. Retrieved March 8, 2015, from http://saphanatutorial.com/column-data-storage-and-row-data-storage-sap-hana/

Schmidt, D. (2014). High Performance Computing with R. Retrieved October 31, 2015, from http://rbigdata.github.io/NIMBioS/presentations/hpcR.pdf

SUSE (2014). CIR food invests in SAP HANA with Migration Savings. Retrieved September 13, 2014, from https://www.suse.com/promo/sap-unix-to-linux/sap6.html

Samy, V. K., Lu, W., Rada, A., Shah, P. B., & Srinivasan, S. (2011). Best practices physical database design for online transaction processing (OLTP) environments. Retrieved May 13, 2014, from http://public.dhe.ibm.com/software/dw/data/bestpractices/DB2BP_Physical_Design_OLTP_0412.pdf

Sato, K. (2012). An Inside Look at Google BigQuery [White paper]. Retrieved from https://cloud.google.com/files/BigQueryTechnicalWP.pdf

Schumacher, R. (2013). A quick tour of internal authentication and authorization security in DataStax Enterprise and Apache Cassandra. Retrieved December 31, 2013, from http://www.datastax.com/dev/blog/a-quick-tour-of-internal-authentication-and-authorization-security-in-datastax-enterprise-and-apache-cassandra

Sebastian-Coleman, L. (2013). In measuring data quality for ongoing improvement: A data quality assessment framework (The Morgan Kaufmann Series on Business Intelligence) (1st edition ed., pp. 28-28). Burlington, Massachusetts: Morgan Kaufmann Publishers.

Sheldon, E. B., & Moore, W. E. (1968). *Indicators of social change: Concepts and measurements.* New York, NY: Russell Sage Foundation.

Singh, V. (2013). Getting Started with Attribute Views in SAP HANA. Retrieved November 27, 2013, from http://www.saphana.com/docs/DOC-3896

Snider, M. (2012). Blu-ray grows, but DVD slide nips home video sales. Retrieved December 30, 2014, from http://usatoday30.usatoday.com/tech/news/story/2012-01-10/blu-ray-sales-2011/52473310/1

Splunk (2015). Splunk® Enterprise. Retrieved November 4, 2015, from http://www.splunk.com/en_us/products/splunk-enterprise.html

Splunk (2015). What is Splunk Enterprise knowledge? Retrieved November 4, 2015, from http://docs.splunk.com/Documentation/Splunk/6.1.4/Knowledge/WhatisSplunkknowledge

Splunk, L. (n.d.). Splunk Advantages - Why to use splunk? Retrieved November 3, 2015, from http://www.learnsplunk.com/splunk-advantages.html

Starschema (2010). Talend SAP component demonstration. Retrieved December 20, 2013, from http://www.slideshare.net/tfoldi/talend-sap-component-demonstration

Steyn, W. (2011). Building Advanced Data Models with SAP HANA. Retrieved November 27, 2013, from http://www.sdn.sap.com/irj/sdn/go/portal/prtroot/docs/library/uuid/6056911a-07cc-2e10-7a8a-ffa9b8cf579c?overridelayout=true

Stolte, C. (2015). History in the making. Retrieved November 1, 2015, from https://careers.tableau.com/ourstory

Tableau (2015). Tableau. Retrieved November 1, 2015, from http://www.tableau.com/products

Tableau (n.d.). All data sources. Retrieved November 1, 2015, from http://www.tableau.com/solutions/data-sources

Theroux-Benoni, D., & Moerski, P. (2014, April 1). *SAP BW 7.4 Launch: Molson Coors Provides a New Approach to Data Warehousing with SAP BW 7.4 Powered by SAP HANA* [Video file]. Retrieved from http://sapinsider.wispubs.com/Assets/Videos/2014/April/BW-74-Launch-Molson-Coors

Thomas, H., & Datta, A. (2001). A conceptual model and algebra for on-line analytical processing in decision support databases. *Information Systems Research, 12*(1), 83-102.

Top500 Org (2013). CHINA'S TIANHE-2 SUPERCOMPUTER TAKES NO. 1 RANKING ON 41ST TOP500 LIST. Retrieved December 7, 2014, from http://www.top500.org/blog/lists/2013/06/press-release/

Venter, C. (2013). Genome sequencing. Retrieved August 4, 2014, from http://www.genomenewsnetwork.org/resources/whats_a_genome/Chp2_1.shtml

Visen, S.S. (2015). Which compression types exist?. Retrieved April 10, 2015, from http://www.stechies.com/which-compression-types-exist/

Vries, A. D. (2015). How many packages are there really on CRAN? Retrieved October 31, 2015, from http://blog.revolutionanalytics. com/2015/06/how-many-packages-are-there-really-on-cran.html

Wallace, D. (2011). 4 Ways to Prevent Dirty Data From Spoiling Analytics. Retrieved November 27, 2013, from http://spotfire. tibco.com/blog/?p=5750

Wallace, D. (2011). How "Dirty Data" Derails Your Company's Data Analytics and ROI. Retrieved November 27, 2013, from http:// spotfire.tibco.com/blog/?p=5631

Weintraub, A. (2014). Big Pharma Opens Up Its Big Data. Retrieved August 1, 2014, from http://www.technologyreview.com/ news/529046/big-pharma-opens-up-its-big-data/

White, A. (2012). How People Spend Their Time Online [Infographic]. Retrieved December 18, 2013, from http://www. go-gulf.com/blog/online-time/

White, A. (2012). How People Spend Their Time Online [Infographic]. Retrieved December 18, 2013, from http://alexwhite.org/2012/05/ infographic-how-people-spend-their-time-online/

Wickham, H. (2015). Memory. Retrieved October 31, 2015, from http://adv-r.had.co.nz/memory.html

Woodie, A. (2013). The Big Data Market By the Numbers. Retrieved December 10, 2013, from http://www.datanami.com/2013/10/03/ the_big_data_market_by_the_numbers/

Woodie, A. (2015). Why Gartner Dropped Big Data Off the Hype Curve. Retrieved November 1, 2015, from http://www.datanami. com/2015/08/26/why-gartner-dropped-big-data-off-the-hype-curve/

Willamette University (n.d.). Computation in the brain. Retrieved December 7, 2014, from http://www.willamette.edu/~gorr/ classes/cs449/brain.html

Yegulalp, S. (2015). SQL Server 2016 gets an R (language) rating. Retrieved October 31, 2015, from http://www.infoworld.com/ article/2998648/sql/sql-server-2016-gets-an-r-language-rating. html

Yoo, S., Lee, K. H., Lee, H. J., Ha, K., Lim, C., Chin, H. J., ... Cho, E. Y. (2012). Seoul National University Bundang Hospital's Electronic System for Total Care. Retrieved July 27, 2014, from http://www.ncbi.nlm.nih.gov/pmc/articles/PMC3402557/

Yuhana, N., Kisker, H., & Murphy, D. (2013). Case study: Maple Leaf Foods relies on SAP HANA to enable faster business analytics. Retrieved September 14, 2014, from http://www.saphana. com/docs/DOC-4201

Zhang, S. (2014). Big pharma plus big data could equal big savings. Retrieved August 1, 2014, from http://news.medill.northwestern. edu/chicago/news.aspx?id=228875

Appendix A

Oversized Tables

Table A1

SAP HANA Performance - Consumer products, food, and beverages

Corporation	Prior to SAP HANA	After SAP HANA	ROI
Red Bull	1.5 TB database	0.3 TB database	N.A.
CIR Food	Reports required 20 minutes.	Few seconds	70%
Maple Leaf Foods	500 business analytics reports.	Reduced to 25 reports, running under a seconds.	N.A.
Molson Coors	Prototype reports required two weeks; delta data loads took 20 minutes, and required the use of a 4.6 TB Oracle database. Oracle database size of 4.6 TB	Prototype reports required one day, delta data loads took 2 seconds. ODS activations have shown 70% to 80% reduction in terms of time. SAP HANA database size of 900 GB. 80.9% of database reduction. SAP BW cube loading improved by 10 times.	N.A.
Frucor	N.A.	900GB SAP HANA database with a 511% of reduction in data compression ratio. BW queries ran 10-100 times faster. Data loads ran 5-10 times faster than before. Database size of 150 GB. Database size of 100 GB.	N.A.
Magazine zum Globus AG	Database size of 550 GB	Accelerated data loading by 70%.	N.A.
SHS Group Ltd.	Database size of 661 GB		100% ROI in 2 to 3 years.

Table A1

SAP HANA Performance - Consumer products, food, and beverages

Corporation	Prior to SAP HANA	After SAP HANA	ROI
Frucor	N.A.	900GB SAP HANA database with a 511% of reduction in data compression ratio. BW queries ran 10-100 times faster. Data loads ran 5-10 times faster than before.	N.A.
Magazine zum Globus AG	Database size of 550 GB.	Database size of 150 GB.	N.A.
SHS Group Ltd.	Database size of 661 GB.	Database size of 100 GB. Accelerated data loading by 70% .	100% ROI in 2 to 3 years.

Table A2

SAP HANA Performance –Automotive, discrete manufacturing, energy and natural resources, financial services, public services, healthcare, information technology, high tech, and utilities

Industry or Organization	Implementation	Prior to SAP HANA	After SAP HANA
Utilities	SAP BW 7.3	DSO activation required 21 hours 40 minutes for 5.2 million records.	DSO reduced to 40 minutes.
		4.3 TB database	0.7 TB database
		Query execution required 471 seconds.	Query execution required 1 second.
		Infocubes required 90 minutes to be populated.	Infocubes required 30 minutes to be populated.
Automotive	SAP BW 7.3	N.A.	Optimization of SAP HANA InfoCubes improved by 1.39 times. DSO activation improved by 4.15 times. Query execution time improved by 8.5 times. BW Webl reports execution time improved by 11.6 times. HANA optimized InfoCubes have shown a response time improvement by 45 times; that has an improvement rate by 26 times.

Table A2

SAP HANA Performance –Automotive, discrete manufacturing, energy and natural resources, financial services, public services, healthcare, information technology, high tech, and utilities

SAP	SAP HANA	Database size 7.1TB	Database size 1.8TB
Lenovo	SAP BW/SAP HANA	N.A.	Report performance by 20 times. Data compression by 2 times.
Nissha	SAP BW/SAP HANA		
Seoul's National University Hospital	Microsoft BESTCare 2.0 and SAP HANA	Batch processing of 7 hours.	SAP BW query performance improved by 60 times.
		Generation of reports in 346.6 seconds	Batch processing of 2 hours. 71.4% improvement of batch processing. Generation of reports in 1.8 seconds. Improvement of 99.4%.
		Data extraction in 30 minutes to 1 hour for data of 3 to 6 months range. Usage of third-line of antibiotics 5.8% times.	Data extraction of 10 years' worth of data was retrieved in 2 to 3 seconds. Usage of third-line of antibiotics 1.2% and subsequently no third-line antibiotics.

Table A2

SAP HANA Performance –Automotive, discrete manufacturing, energy and natural resources, financial services, public services, healthcare, information technology, high tech, and utilities

Industry or Organization	Implementation	Prior to SAP HANA	After SAP HANA
Charité Universitätsmedizin Berlin	SAP BW 7.3 and SAP BOBJ 4.1	N.A.	Query executing requiring only a few seconds using a 20TB database.
Kardinal Schwarzenberg Hospital	SAP ERP IS-healthcare, SAP HANA	Database size of 760 GB.	Database size of 430 GB.
Mitsui Knowledge Industry	SAP ERP, SAP HANA, R, and Hadoop	N.A.	Performance was enhanced approximately by a factor of 408,000.
Medtronic	SAP BW and BOBJ	BOBJ report execution required 3 hours.	BOBJ report execution required 3 minutes.
City of Boston	SAP BOBJ	Backlog of 600 pending permits.	Reduction of pending permits to 10 and an observed increase in emergency call monitoring.
Fire and rescue NSW	SAP HANA	Database size of 750 GB.	Database size of 220 GB.

Table A2

SAP HANA Performance –Automotive, discrete manufacturing, energy and natural resources, financial services, public services, healthcare, information technology, high tech, and utilities

Industry or Organization	Implementation	Prior to SAP HANA	After SAP HANA
Honeywell Aerospace	SAP BOBJ and HANA	Extraction from 5 TB of data required 12 hours.	Extraction from 5 TB of data required less than one minute.
Sagem	SAP BW	Required a 2.15 TB RDBMS.	Required a 443 GB database.

Table A3

Big data in healthcare industry

Component	Size
Single genome	50 MB
Global genome database	15 PB
Medical prescriptions	100 GB
Per-scan medical image	10 GB

Notes. Values present minimum estimates.

Table A4

Top big data catalysts for business intelligence

Catalyst	%
Big data driven operational research	30.1
Big data driven consumer trend and behavior analysis	29.7
Point of sales analysis	20.6
Big data driven innovations	18.8
Sensor data processing	17.0
NoSQL analytics	11.0

Table A5

SAP Certified hardware vendors for SAP HANA

Partner	Hardware Configuration
Cisco	Unified computing system with high-performance blade server B440 M2 model. A combination of either two or four Intel Xeon E7-4870 and 8880 processors with a maximum of 16 nodes. Maximum 8 TB RAM with 16 x 512 GB. EMC VNX5300 family storage (up to 90 TB). Microchip file system. SUSE Linux enterprise server 11 SP1. Unified computing system with B440 M2 model blade server- four Intel Xeon E7-4870 servers and node - (maximum 16 nodes). Up to 8TB RAM (16 x 512GB). NetApp FAS3240 storage series can expand up to 115.2 TB network file system. SUSE Linux Enterprise Server 11 SP1.
Fujitsu	Primergy server RX600 S6 quad socket - four Intel Xeon E7-4870 rack server and node - maximum 16 nodes. Up to 8TB RAM (16 x 512GB). Fujitsu Eternus disk storage system with NR1000 F3240 storage (maximum memory of 115.2TB).Network file system. SUSE Linux Enterprise Server 11 for SAP Applications.
Hitachi	Hitachi computer blade server 2000 –four Intel Xeon E7-8870 servers and node - maximum 16 nodes. Maximum 8TB RAM (16 x 512GB). Hitachi virtual storage platform (maximum 120 TB). Third extended file system. SUSE Linux enterprise server 11 SP1 for SAP Applications. Disaster recovery solution certified by SAP in a scale-out storage replication. Compute blade server 2000 – eight Intel Xeon E7-8870 server and node - (maximum 16 nodes). Maximum 16TB RAM. Hitachi virtual storage platform (maximum 120 TB). Extended file system. Storage replication with certified disaster recovery solution. SUSE Linux Enterprise Server 11 SP2 for SAP Applications.
HP	HP ProLiant BL680c G7 - four Intel Xeon E7-4870 processors and nodes - (maximum 16 nodes). Maximum 8TB RAM (16 x 512GB). HP P6500 Enterprise virtual array storage (up to 115.2TB). Network file system with HP X9300 segmented, scalable Network storage gateway. SLES 11 for SAP applications.
IBM	Workload optimized X3950 x5 – eight Intel Xeon E7-8870 processors and node - (maximum 16 nodes). Maximum 16TB RAM. SUSE Linux enterprise server 11 for SAP Applications.

Appendix B

List of Acronyms

A and D.	Aerospace and Defense.
ABAP.	Advanced business application programming language.
ACID.	Atomicity, consistency, isolation, durability.
AFL.	Application function library.
ALE.	Application link enabling.
AOF.	Append only file.
API.	Application programming interface.
ASL.	Application specific licensing.
ATP.	Available-to-promise.
BEx.	Business explorer.
BI.	Business intelligence.
BOBJ.	Business objects.
BODS.	Business objects data services.
BSON.	Binary JavaScript Object Notation.
BW.	Business information warehouse.
BWA.	Business information warehouse accelerator.

C4ISR.	Command, Control, Communications, Computers, Intelligence, Surveillance, and Reconnaissance.
CAGR.	Compound annual growth rate.
CD.	Compact disc.
CDO.	Chief data officer.
CIA.	Central Intelligence Agency.
CIO.	Chief information officer.
CNN.	Cable news network.
CO-PA.	Controlling and profitability analysis.
CPU.	Central processing unit.
CODASYL.	Conference on data systems language.
COPA.	Controlling and profitability analysis.
CRM.	Customer relationship management.
CT.	Computer tomography.
CTI.	Computer telephony integration.
DB2.	Database 2.
DDP.	Dual die package.
DHL.	Dalsey, Hillblom, & Lynn.
DLR.	Deutsche Luft-Reederei.
DNA.	Deoxyribonucleic acid.
DOD.	Department of Defense.
DRAM.	Dynamic random access memory.
DSO.	Data store object.
DVD.	Digital video disc.
EMC.	When the EMC Corporation was founded, they named it based on $E = MC^2$ equation.
EMR.	Amazon Elastic MapReduce.
EMR.	Electronic medical records.
ERP.	Enterprise resource planning.
ETL.	Extract, transform, and load.

FDA.	Federal Drug Administration.
FI-AP.	SAP Financials-accounting-payables.
FI-AR.	SAP Financials-accounting-receivables.
FiOS.	Fiber optic services.
FSCM.	Financial supply chain management.
Gb.	Gigabits.
GDP.	Gross domestic product.
GHz.	Gigahertz.
GPS.	Global positioning system.
HDFS.	Hadoop distributed file system.
HP.	Hewlett-Packard.
HR.	Human resources management.
HT.	Hyper-threading.
HTTP.	Hypertext transfer protocol.
IBM.	International Business Machines Corporation.
ICT.	Information, communications, and technology.
IDC.	International Data Corporation.
IDM.	Identity management.
IDoc.	Intermediate document.
IMDB.	in-memory database.
IMS.	IBM Information management system.
IM.	Inventory management.
IMDB.	In-memory database.
IOT.	Internet of Things.
IQ.	Intellectual quotient.
IS.	Industrial solutions.
IS-P.	Industrial solutions for pharmaceuticals.
IT.	Information technology.
IVR.	Interactive Voice Response.
JSON.	JavaScript Object Notation.
MB.	Megabytes

MDM.	Master data management.
mIOT.	Medical Internet of things.
MM.	Materials Management.
MOLAP.	Multidimensional online analytical processing.
MSSQL.	Microsoft Structured Query Language.
MTV.	Music Television.
RDBMS.	Relational database management system
R&D.	Research and development.
RDS.	Rapid deployment solutions.
ReRAM.	Resistive random access memory.
RESTful.	Representational State Transfer.
RFID.	Remote frequency identifier.
RLANG.	R language.
RODBC.	R language open database connection.
ROI.	Return on investment.
ROLAP.	Relational online analytical processing.
SABRE.	Semi-automated business research environment
SAP.	Systems, applications, and products in data processing.
SAP HANA.	Systems, applications, and products - High-performance analytic appliance.
SAS.	Statistical analysis system.
SCM.	Supply chain management.
SD.	Sales and distribution.
SE.	Societas Europaea.
SEQUEL.	Structured English QUEry language.
SGI.	Silicon Graphics, Inc.
SID.	Stammdaten Identifikationsnummer.
SIMD.	Single instruction, multiple data.
SLD.	System landscape directory.
SLT.	SAP landscape transformation.

SMD.	Solution manager diagnostics.
SMP.	Symmetric multiprocessing.
SMP.	SAP Mobile platform.
SPS.	Support pack stack.
SQL.	Structured-query language.
SQL3.	Structured-query language 3.
SRM.	Supplier-relationship management.
SSD.	Solid-state drive.
STT-RAM.	Spin-transfer torque random access memory.
SUSE.	Software und System Entwicklung.
TB.	Terabytes.
TCO.	Total cost of ownership.
TPM.	Trade promotion management.
TSV.	Through-silicon via.
TV.	Television.
UD.	Universal data.
UID.	Unique identification project.
US.	United States of America.

ENDNOTES

1   Rider, F. (1944). *The Scholar and the Future of the Research Library. A Problem and Its Solution*. New York, NY: Hadham Press.

2   Moore, W. E., & Sheldon, E. B. (1968). *Indicators of Social Change: Concepts and Measurements by Eleanor Bernert Sheldon, Wilbert E. Moore (1968) Hardcover*. New York, NY: Russell Sage Foundation.

3   Sebastian-Coleman, L. (2013). In measuring data quality for ongoing improvement: A data quality assessment framework (The Morgan Kaufmann Series on Business Intelligence) (1st edition ed., pp. 28-28). Burlington, Massachusetts: Morgan Kaufmann Publishers.

4   Price, D. (1961). *Science Since Babylon*. New Haven, CT: Yale University Press.

5   Price, D. J. (1975). *Science since Babylon*. New Haven, CT: Yale University Press.

6   Codd, E. F. (1970). A relational model of data for large shared data banks. Retrieved January 12, 2015, from http://www.seas.upenn.edu/~zives/03f/cis550/codd.pdf

7   Acharjya, D. P., Dehuri, S., & Sanyal, S. (2015). *Computational Intelligence for Big Data Analysis: Frontier Advances and Applications (Adaptation, Learning, and Optimization)*. New York, NY: Springer.

8   Lyman, P., & Varian, H. R. (2000, December). How much information? The journal of electronic publishing, 6. http://dx.doi.org/http://dx.doi.org/10.3998/3336451.0006.204

9   Neuman, W. L. (2003). *Social Research Methods: Qualitative and Quantitative Approaches* (5th ed.). Boston, MA: Pearson Education, Inc.

10 Creswell, J. W. (2012). Educational research: Planning, conducting, and evaluating quantitative and qualitative research (4th ed.). Boston, MA: Pearson Education, Inc

11 Neuman, W. L. (2011). *Basics of Social Research: Qualitative and Quantitative Approaches* (3rd ed.). Boston, MA: Pearson Education Inc.

12 Kelly, S. M. (2012). Google Fiber TV Coming Soon to a Living Room Near You. Retrieved February 23, 2013, from http://mashable.com/2012/07/26/google-fiber-tv-/#4Bu1RAfr1mqp

13 Jones, K. (1998). An introduction to data warehousing: What are the implications for the Network? *International Journal of Network Management*, 8, 42-56.

14 Bontempo, C., & Zagelow, G. (1998, September 1). The IBM data warehouse architecture. *Communications of the ACM, 41*(9), 38-48. http://dx.doi.org/10.1145/285070.285078

15 Thomas, H., & Datta, A. (2001). A conceptual model and algebra for on-line analytical processing in decision support databases. *Information Systems Research, 12*(1), 83-102.

16 Howson,C.(2013).7topbusinessintelligencetrendsfor2013.Retrieved May 26, 2013, from http://www.informationweek.com/software/business-intelligence/7-top-business-intelligence-trends-for-2/240146994

17 Plattner, H. (2009). A common database approach for OLTP and OLAP using an in-memory column database. Retrieved May 7, 2014, from http://www.sigmod09.org/images/sigmod1ktp-plattner.pdf

18 Azevedo, F. A., Carvalho, L. R., Grinberg, L. T., Farfel, J. M., Leite, R. E., Jacob, W. F., & Herculano-Houzel, S. (2009). Equal numbers of neuronal and nonneuronal cells make the human brain an isometrically scaled-up primate brain. Retrieved December 7, 2014, from http://www.ncbi.nlm.nih.gov/pubmed/19226510